COMPUTER MONOGRAPHS

10

EXECUTIVE PROGRAMS AND OPERATING SYSTEMS

EXECUTIVE PROGRAMS AND OPERATING SYSTEMS

edited by

G. CUTTLE
&
P. B. ROBINSON

MACDONALD: LONDON
AND
AMERICAN ELSEVIER INC.: NEW YORK

First published 1970

Sole distributors for the United States and Dependencies
American Elsevier Publishing Company, Inc.
52 Vanderbilt Avenue
New York N.Y. 10017

Sole Distributors for the British Isles and Commonwealth
Macdonald & Co. (Publishers) Ltd
49–50 Poland Street
London W.1

All remaining areas
Elsevier Publishing Company
P.O. Box 211
Jan van Galenstraat 335
Amsterdam
The Netherlands

British SBN 356 028046
American SBN 444 19690 0
Library of Congress Catalog Card No. 73–107785

Printed in Great Britain
by Balding & Mansell
London and Wisbech

NOTE TO THE AMERICAN READER

The use of the term 'Executive' is a British one, analagous to the American 'Supervisor'. Since the British 1900 Series is extensively used in the book for illustrative purposes it seemed sensible to use the native term, and the American reader can interpret it as 'Supervisor' wherever it occurs without loss of meaning.

CONTENTS

PREFACE

Executives and Operating Systems represent a rapidly developing aspect of systems programming. At the time of writing most of the more highly developed systems have only been released for general use for a relatively short time, and very few large systems (Atlas Supervisor is one) can be regarded as having passed through all the stages of enhancement into their final, fully developed, forms. Consequently there is still a considerable variety of different approaches among the various implementors and although a clear picture is emerging of the spectrum of facilities which operating systems will provide, there is still scope for considerable speculation as to how this will best be achieved. Thus in preparing this book we were faced with two major problems. First, should we attempt to describe all the approaches generally, or concentrate on one? Second, should we confine ourselves to those aspects which are well established, or attempt to convey the variety of thoughts among those involved with current developments as well? To both problems we have sought a compromise solution. To allow us to pursue some topics in reasonable depth, we have concentrated on one series of operating systems: the George systems for 1900, but have included chapters both to relate this to one of the principal alternative approaches, and to cover one aspect, real-time, which calls for facilities not present in George. The selection of the 1900 systems as a base for the book was partly convenience—both editors work for ICL—and partly because its stage of development was particularly appropriate for our purposes in that George 1 and 2, which contain the simpler facilities, are fully developed whereas at the time of writing George 3 was still in its last stages of development and thus gave the opportunity to include the latest thoughts on the more advanced facilities.

To allow us to embrace a variety of thoughts, we have adopted an editorial approach so that the book comprises chapters written by a number of different authors all of whom have been actively involved in different aspects of executive and operating systems work. For obvious reasons they have generally been drawn from ICL, but we have deliberately tried to select them from different locations within the company so as to obtain as wide a cross-section as possible. Naturally this has resulted in a corresponding variety of styles and views, but we hope that any apparent inconsistency that results is compensated by an understanding of the continuing and varied new thinking which is a characteristic of this field of development today.

Finally, apart from our considerable thanks to the authors of our chapters, we should like to thank Colin Merton for many helpful suggestions, Elizabeth Vickers, the ICL Librarian at Lily Hill, Bracknell, for compiling lists of background literature, and Diana Dunstan and Cheryl Pull for their patient and accurate typing of much amended drafts.

G. Cuttle
P. B. Robinson
November 1969

1

INTRODUCTION TO OPERATING SYSTEM CONCEPTS

MARTIN WARWICK

To introduce the concepts of Operating Systems Martin Warwick first considers the question 'Why have an Operating System?' He traces their historical development through to the three main types today, Batch, Multiaccess and Real Time. Then he considers who, in a computer environment, needs operating systems and discusses their particular requirements. Finally he discusses the costs of an operating system and what makes a good one.

1.1 Introduction

The importance of operating systems has only been recently recognised and accepted. In a modern installation the creation of a consistent operating environment is as important as the computer itself. The recognition of this fact has led to a series of manufacturer-supplied operating systems of which the more advanced have reduced human intervention in the control of a computer to minor proportions and then only of a trivial nature. The operating system of any computer installation is the organisation and the method of running the computer, and it involves a variety of people, equipment, and programs. While in this book we are concerned mainly with operations which the computer itself controls or directs, we must bear in mind the overall picture of the complete installation operation. No installation is yet fully automated, but as the complexity of computers grows and their speed increases so the requirement for automation is of greater importance. The operating system that a manufacturer supplies is only the basis on which a complete organisation can be built.

In this chapter we shall look at the overall requirements for an operating system, but this does not imply that any single system should contain them all; each one has to be designed to make the best use of the available resources of an installation, people, equipment and time. The analysis of a system requires answers to some fundamental questions. Why have an operating system? Who needs it and for doing what? What does it cost? What makes a good operating system? The systems described in later chapters should be viewed in the light of the answers to these questions.

1.2 Why have an Operating System?

The early computers were no more than useful pieces of hardware, and each job they executed was interfaced straight to the machine operations. Each programmer was a machine expert, a person who understood every eccentricity of the computer and worked the switches. As libraries of useful routines were built up and became of general use within an installation, the operation became more standardised and more amenable to the use of a permanent operator who could learn to handle standard work. The programmer, providing he kept to various conventions, could save himself time and trouble by using standard routines to perform common operations. The operator supervised the machine, looked after cards, paper tape, magnetic tape and printer output, and kept a record of who was using the computer and for what. The speed of the machine was slow and efficiency in operation was of minor importance. But when the first generation of computers were replaced by a second with a speed differential of up to one hundred times, new problems arose. In particular, because of the great increase in speed operational inefficiencies could no longer be discounted, unless each job was a long one. If it takes five minutes to set up a job which runs for two hours, only a little over 4 per cent of the useful computer time is wasted. If, however, it takes five minutes to set up a short arithmetic type calculation which runs for thirty seconds, virtually the whole day is consumed by operating overheads and the computer is being used very wastefully. With such jobs the case for automating the job set-up by letting the machine control it is very strong.

As soon as control of the machine is shared between the operator and the machine itself, however, further difficulties arise. The programmer can misuse the machine without the operator knowing it by altering the sequence of calling the next job, or by using tapes illegally and so on. These sorts of difficulties can only be overcome when personal control of a program by the programmer is replaced by the impersonal control of an operating system.

So the concept of a two-level machine having an interrupt or supervisory level, and a user level, was introduced. Under certain conditions the hardware could switch its instruction execution from the sequence dictated by the user job to that of a supervisory program. The conditions might be, for example, attempts to execute certain types of instructions which the system itself wished to control, or trapping misuse of the hardware, or intervention after so many instructions or after a certain time. Using these devices the system can monitor precisely the conduct of the user program. It can place time restraints on a user and trap program errors, and it can also generate messages to tell the operator the actions it is performing and what external actions are required.

In addition to the increase in execution speed of second generation computers their input-output units were able to operate autonomously and in parallel with instruction processing. Advantage of this was taken in two ways: firstly, all programs had now to be written, so far as possible, in such a way that instruction processing was always done while input-output operations were proceeding, which required conventional double buffering techniques and the balancing of data transfers against the time required for processing: secondly, multiprogramming was introduced. On a two-level machine it is possible for the supervisory program to be told when a user job is held up waiting for the completion of an input-output transfer. If a second user job is resident in the computer it may as well use the processor until the first job is ready to recommence. This is known as multiprogramming and is the sharing of several autonomous processing units between several user jobs. In many second-generation computers it was called timesharing, but this term is now generally accepted as referring to multiaccess.

For a two-level machine a resident control program was required and this was variously called Executive, Supervisor, Director, Master Routine, Master Control Program. With these resident programs the power of operating systems grew. The user no longer had the option of conforming, or not, to the conventions of the system, conformity was enforced by the resident package. The operating system could now dictate the conduct of programs, which programs were loaded and in which order; it could trap actions, terminate programs, limit programs' and programmers' use of store, peripheral devices and time.

Thanks to the power of the resident control program, automatic control of an installation became a possibility. Control of a computer system was no longer in the hands of a user but in the hands of the operating system writer. An artificial interface was imposed between the user and the machine hardware, and any job not fitting the interface, whether in its job control details or program, would not run. The resident control programs placed an 'authoritarian seal' on operating systems. No one could bypass their actions or effects. To the computer user they define the machine hardware.

The third generation of computers has encouraged the further exploitation of principles developed on the more advanced of the second-generation machines. The desire for less human intervention and to make the task of the user simpler has considerably increased the size and activities of operating systems. The hardware has receded further and further from the user and the operating system has taken its place. To each type of user it presents an interface. To the programmer, in many cases, it is a high-level language—the logical structure of files, and a job description system. Present operating systems can be roughly categorised into three types, and of course combinations of the three.

The first is known as a *Batch* operating system, taking its name from its manner of use. A batch of jobs is fed in and processed one by one in an order selected by the operating system, usually under multiprogramming. An operating system of this type takes many facilities away from the user that the early computer provided. The user has his job swallowed by the system and is later presented with results in terms of manipulated files and line printer hard copy. The first generation user watched his program run, watched it go wrong, entered new parameters to alter its course, performed on-line correction.

The second type of system, *Multiaccess*, enables this machine contact to be re-established. Each user is given an input-output terminal of some kind, a Teletype or Video Display Unit, and the available processing power is shared out between all the users. Each new system or extension to an old one creates new problems. The connection of terminals is one. In general their servicing differs from that of conventional input-output devices and is generally performed through a special multiplexing processor or unit. Also the sharing of the system amongst so many users provides large problems in the use of core store and of backing store files. With so many users the security of data is of prime importance. Such considerations lead to the creation of a far more elaborate and automated system than is normally required for batched operation.

The third type is known as *Real Time*. Real Time describes a situation in which the actions are required to be executed in an interval which is realistic in terms of human reaction time. It may appear that the definition of a Real Time system is much the same as that of a Multiaccess system. In practice two totally different things are meant. In a Multiaccess system a normal set of user jobs is being processed, and every user can be running a different program; 'multiaccess' refers only to the fact that all the users are being given a turn to use the machine resources. In Real Time, on the other hand, most users are operating on the same, single program or small set of programs and the system can therefore be optimised to permit a very high number of users. In general the Real Time user is a clerk, the Multiaccess user is a programmer. There may be 1000 terminals attached to a Real Time system, there are unlikely to be more than 100 attached to a Multiaccess system. A commonly quoted example of a Real Time system is that used for seat reservations on an airline. Real Time problems are discussed in a later chapter. Suffice it to say here that in the present state of the art both Multiaccess and Real Time systems involve features of great complexity, since they are necessarily to a high degree under the control of the computer.

Now let us return to the question which heads this section. Why have an Operating System? Having proceeded so far from the first generation machine it is easy to forget the logical steps which have brought us to our present position.

1. The speed of the computer compared with human speed requires the computer to take decisions previously taken by the the operator.
2. The complexities of modern systems are too great for an operator to control.
3. The users must be controlled at the level of their programs.
4. A central pool of facilities must be provided by the system.

This list is far from exhaustive and other reasons will be presented in the next section.

1.3 Who needs it and for doing what?

The many parties interested in a computer operating system are here listed together with the information and service they require. As stated earlier, not all these things will be provided in any single system. In fact many of the operations can be expected to be carried out economically by a manual process.

1.3.1 The Computer Manager

Main interests: Installation or Complete System Control
Operational Efficiency
System Profitability

1. *Logging all machine activities*
   All operations performed in the system must be recorded. These include the use of files, the actions of the operator, the entering and execution of users' jobs.
2. *Job accounting*
   Apart from the logging of information a method of charging users is needed. The charge is dependent not only on the user's program but on the use it makes of the system with regard to files, facilities and operation.
3. *Job control*
   Some jobs are urgent, others must be finished by a certain deadline, some can be multiprogrammed together. The computer manager wants a system which permits each job to be executed at the right time.
4. *Efficient working of the operating system*
   The latter is an overhead which reduces profitability, and so must be justified by the efficiency it produces.
5. *Security of user jobs*
   Each job must be secure from corruption from outside sources.

Jobs co-resident in core store must not be able to corrupt each other.

6. *Security of files against misuse and accidental corruption*
   The user has entrusted his files on magnetic tape and disc, etc. to the installation. It must be impossible for a user to have access illegally to another's information.
7. *Rapid restart after machine failure*
   Following the inevitable hardware failures a rapid, sometimes immediate restart is required. This should involve the loss of as little work as possible, and the filing system must be consistent so that the work of the installation can continue.

1.3.2 The Computer Operator

Main interest: Control of the machine

1. *Actions to be taken*
   The operator must be informed whenever the operating system requires an action such as loading a file or typing a reply to a request. He needs a consistent method of presenting these messages.
2. *Status of hardware*
   The operator needs to be told which devices are busy, which require loading and when a device requires attention, e.g. a line printer running out of paper.
3. *Status of jobs*
   The operator must also be kept informed about which jobs are running, which have been loaded and the devices they are using, as well as which jobs have ended. The operator must have the power to suspend a job either temporarily or permanently when it clearly goes out of control.
4. *Device loading*
   The operator must be able to mount replaceable volumes such as magnetic tapes or discs on any free drive, and the system should be able to recognise them by their volume names. This is termed Automatic Volume Recognition.

1.3.3 The System User

Main interest: Presentation of a job and its execution

1. *Job Control*
   The user has dual interests. He wants a method of describing a job to the system which is simple to use, and yet he wants a multitude of facilities which express exactly his requirements regarding the deadline or importance of the job, the mode of utilisation of his files, the utilisation of hardware elements such as store or channels, and how long the job is to run.
2. *Presentation of data*
   The user normally has data for a job on cards or paper tape.

This data together with the job control is the external input to the system. The operating system must be able to handle both together if it wishes to stack away complete jobs for later scheduling.

3. *The file system*
   The user must be able to access his magnetic tape and disc files by calling upon them by name. The system is expected to do the user's housekeeping on them, to ensure that previous versions are preserved and that the correct version is used. The security and integrity of files is of utmost importance.
4. *Receipt of results*
   Where results are stored on tape or disc for later printing the operating system has further internal scheduling to perform to ensure that the user gets them as soon as possible.
5. *Multiaccess requirements*
   These are considerably greater. The user is in conversation with the system and his dialogue with the machine must be easily understandable. The system should be conversational in nature, that is, it must be capable of asking and answering questions and of informing the user. It must respond quickly. A host of supporting programs must be available so that the user has every aid to perform his task. The user is not conscious of the work the system has to perform to support the multiaccess image, nor should he be.
6. *Hardware faults*
   The user knows there will be hardware faults but should not have to take any action. The system should be capable of restarting jobs without inconveniencing the user.

1.3.4 The Programmer

Main interest: Developing and testing programs

1. *Using the program testing system*
   Most installations spend a high proportion of computer time testing programs. The sequence and the aids for testing are highly important. These consist of trials systems, compilers, text editors, composers, trace routines etc.
2. *The interface of the operating system to a program*
   The programmer calls upon facilities of the operating system to service records in files, perform input-output operations and macro instructions, allocate core store or backing store. The operating system provides a method for the program to send messages to the operator.
3. *Libraries of useful routines*
   There should be a collection of subroutines together with a simple way of incorporating them in a program.

1.3.5 The Systems Engineer

Main interest: Maintaining and improving the operating system

1. *Ease of modification of the software*
   There must be documentation and flow charting to aid in making corrections or changes, and the software should be modular.
2. *Generating a system*
   New releases of software necessitate the generation of a new operating system from a tape or disc. During this process an operating system is created for a particular installation, the parameters being the amount of core store, peripheral configuration and facilities required.

1.3.6 Maintenance Engineers

Main interest: Early discovery and repair of hardware faults

1. *Notification of faults*
   All hardware faults should be recorded by the system, even those, such as magnetic tape parity failure, which can be remedied by repeated attempts. The maintenance engineer should be able to obtain a complete log of all these.
2. *Diagnosis of faults*
   If a hardware fault is found while software is controlling the machine, the software should attempt to diagnose it so that it can be isolated for quicker repair.

1.3.7 Hardware Designer

Main interest: Hardware interface to the operating system design

1. *Interface to the system*
   The hardware design can influence the design of an operating system and particularly its efficiency. The operating system has to deal with the raw hardware and provide the user with an interface. The way input-output operations are performed and interruptions permitted can have a considerable effect upon the performance of the system as a whole.
2. *Software interpretation of instructions—Extracodes*
   If an operating system is to be applicable to a series of computers covering a wide price range, the hardware designers may want some instructions interpreted by software on the less powerful machines. Or if a facility such as floating point arithmetic is only rarely used it may be economical to implement it by software. In most computers instruction codes not interpreted by hardware can be trapped for servicing by software. In the ICL 1900 range such instructions are called Extracodes, in some other machines the facility is provided by Operation Code Traps.

1.4 What does an Operating System cost a User?

There is no generally accepted method of assessing the cost of an operating system. Hardware has for some time been assessed in terms of instruction mixes, but no similar method has been found for operating systems. A user no longer controls how long a job will take to process; the time is a function of how the operating system schedules its running, the facilities it uses, as well as the object code specifically created by the user. An instruction mix must be replaced by a job mix for measurement, but no agreement can be found for the mix of jobs. A job mix is only relevant to the Batch type system; it is unlikely to be applicable to a multiaccess type. However, it is possible to draw up a credit and debit account for operating systems on the basis of some essential criteria.

On the debit side there are two factors whose expense can be reckoned. Firstly there is the amount of hardware permanently tied to the execution of the operating system. There will be a considerable core utilisation which may vary from 1000 words to 25 000 words, from the simplest system to the most elaborate. In addition there will be some effect upon the backing store, perhaps magnetic tapes, discs or drums. Secondly there is the amount of time taken by operating system actions. These two factors are measurable, although the second, the amount of time, may be disguised by the operating system writers and directly accounted to the job rather than separately declared. Apart from these measurable quantities there may be a certain nuisance factor. The operating system is the only interface the user has with the computer. It cannot be by-passed and the user is completely bound to stay within its purlieu. The user may be inconvenienced by its conventions and facilities. It may be a system which is far too general for his specialised use, yet he is forced to suffer its inefficiencies. Another debit commonly suffered, especially by the early users of the system, is the number of flaws in the software, and the more elaborate the system becomes, the more flaws it may have in its early stages.

On the credit side there are the facilities the system provides. It is easy to lose sight of the importance of these and forget the difficulties of working to a hardware rather than a software interface. An operating system should provide a significant increase in the total throughput of a computer, that is, the number of jobs it can process, and a real saving in time, and hence money.

But overriding all considerations of credit and debit is the question —could an installation operate without an operating system? In any complex operation a point is reached where a machine is absolutely necessary. A human being cannot take, within an acceptable time, many of the decisions that an operating system makes. The operating system is working at about 10 000 times the reaction speed of a manual operator. Again, can a system without some file security be envisaged nowadays?

A present-day user does not buy a piece of hardware. He buys a computer package consisting of hardware, an operating system, applications packages and other software. The operating system is an essential element of the total computer package.

1.5 What makes a good Operating System?

The success of an operating system depends to a great degree on the environment in which it is used. One that is good for one user in providing the right facilities and a useful operating strategy may be far from successful for another user with a different work load. There are many general operating systems which provide functions which would satisfy every type of user, but each function represents an overhead of store utilisation and execution time which restricts the efficiency of the complete system.

The effectiveness of an operating system is thus a function of:

1. *Efficiency*

   A measure of the cost of the overhead of using the system can be represented in terms of storage utilisation and in the ratio

$$1 - \frac{\text{time spent in Operating System housekeeping}}{\text{total time the system is in use}}$$

2. *Functions and facilities*

   The system must be capable of performing all the functions required of it. It must not stop the user from performing logically possible operations.

3. *Ease of use*

   It must be simple to use and must not involve major problems of comprehension, or data preparation.

Successful systems depend on a well-chosen balance between facilities and efficiency. In achieving this balance various compromises have to be made. In a manufacturer's system supplied for general applications across a large market the accent is on facilities and the system is rarely optimised for any specialised work load. In a specialised system a far finer balance can be achieved, with a greater accent on efficiency. In the manufacturers' case a further consideration is that of compatibility across a machine range and with previous or parallel systems. Every user would like an operating system moulded to his own philosophies and needs, but the production cost is so great that only rarely can such an individual package be created and supplied.

2
THE ROLE OF EXECUTIVE PROGRAMS

BRIAN MILLIS

From the general we now turn to the particular. In order that we can consider one family of operating systems in reasonable detail we shall examine those for the ICL 1900 series, and Brian Millis opens the story with Executive, the heart of all the 1900 series systems and, on smaller machines, a modest operating system in its own right. He pursues in greater detail some of the historical background mentioned by Martin Warwick, and introduces the important concepts of parallel processing—multiprogramming, off-lining, subprogramming, multi-access and peripheral interrupts.

2.1 Introduction

This chapter is about 'Executive' programs. As was explained in 1.2, an Executive is a resident control program for a computing system; its function is to control the running of all other programs using the system and to provide various facilities which they can call up. Executives have become increasingly prominent over the last ten years, and in this chapter we shall be looking at the reasons behind this and what in essence an Executive is.

2.2 Software

The development of software through subroutines was mentioned in 1.2, but to really understand the particular place Executives have in relation to hardware on one hand and more general software on the other it is useful to consider this in greater detail. A general-purpose digital computer is capable of performing a comparatively small number of elemental functions; it derives its power from its ability to perform a very large number of such operations on many pieces of data, extremely fast, and from its ability to vary the operations done according to tests carried out on the data. While the stringing together of half a dozen of these elemental operations requires no great degree of intelligence, the number required to do a job of any significance is so large that the quality of the effort needed is changed.

Moreover the limited size of quickly accessible storage available means that the complexity is further aggravated by the need to keep the totality of these strings (the 'program') small, and hence to re-use given elements as often as possible. To produce a program which does the job efficiently, and to get it working becomes an intellectual exercise of some difficulty, and hence very early in the history of computers, the value of designed and working programs was realised. If in a program an operation was needed which had already been programmed in an existing one, the advantage if you could copy across the same coding was so great that it became worth deliberately building up libraries of program sections ('subroutines') which performed various commonly required functions. (The subroutine library for EDSAC 1 at Cambridge University pioneered this approach.)

It was also soon found that in addition to providing larger chunks of program to perform significant functions, the programmer's job could be eased by allowing him to write using operations more complex than the simple ones available as the elemental functions of the machine, and then mechanically translating what was so written into the greater number of elemental operations that achieved the same effect. Hence, of course, are derived higher-level languages and compilers.

Once these things had become established, the machine designer could indeed be allowed to make the elemental functions even less convenient for the programmer to use if this helped him to make the machine cheaper or faster. The unpleasantness of these functions could be hidden from the programmer who would only write in a higher-level language, or, where the awkward functions were concerned with one class of operations (for example, reading from or writing to external media) would always use subroutines to do these. Of course the relevant compilers or subroutines must be written using the less pleasant functions, but, in principle, this need only be done once, and hence one can afford to have them written by highly skilled people.

Having taken this approach, the compilers and subroutines become a necessary part of the system, since for the normal user they are as necessary as the electronics in the machine. The word 'software' has been coined to describe these programs, the 'software' being that collection of programs which must be added to the physical machine, the 'hardware', to make it a viable system for the normal user.

As with most things there are drawbacks. Compiling a program or building it out of general-purpose subroutines almost inevitably does not give as efficient or compact a result as the best possible program tailor made from elemental functions. Because they are general purpose, the subroutine will not for instance do just what you want and no more. This discovery causes many programmers to react against general-purpose software at some stage of their programming life, often to the extent of totally discounting its potential advantages.

The use of sub-assemblies is commonplace in 'hardware' engineering in all fields, including computers. Here, however, it has come to be accepted at least as much because of the reduction on costs achieved by quantity manufacture. Unfortunately for the programmer the cost of the physical program (a punched pack of cards say) is comparatively small and the extra cost of taking more space and time on each run due to using common sub-assemblies has to be offset completely by the savings in design cost and time. So there is often justification for using elemental functions to get the best possible program for some critical part of a job. But this is becoming rarer as the jobs become more complex and the price of a computer of any given speed goes down while that for a programmer does not. We have not yet quite reached the stage where on most machines programming in near-machine code is forbidden; but by now it is common for normal program only to be able to drive peripheral devices through the subroutines of Executive.

When the normal user only sees the machine 'through software', that software is for him part of the machine. If he has the functions he wants performed at the speeds he needs he becomes uninterested in what is done by hardware and what by software. They merge into a common whole. This is most obvious in the case of microprogrammed machines, where the functions used by the programmer are interpreted and performed by an underlying program, the 'microprogram', which uses a very primitive order code implemented in electronic logic. This is the ultimate, in a way, of all programs being built out of subroutines. In practice, the microprogram is usually 'wired' into a special fast read-only store and it is quite impossible for normal programs to use the elementary machine code directly. The programmer does not regard it as the machine code at all, but thinks of the interpreted code (which is usually as low level as the average 'machine code' anyway) as the machine code of this machine. Microprogramming, therefore, is a case of very low-level software which has got so extreme as to go 'hard'. Many of the subroutines in an Executive are analogous to microprogram, but at a slightly higher level and still just 'soft' in the sense that they are in store which can be written to. Executive is thus an extreme form of software and functions performed by it can again be regarded as part of the machine code by normal programmers.

2.3 Parallel Processing

The specific need which Executive and Operating Systems have been devised to fill is to make better use of the computer system—to get more jobs through in a given time. Special purpose systems concentrate on the characteristics of a particular type of job to achieve this for a multitude of such jobs, an example is given by the special systems for doing small student programs written in FORTRAN. In this chapter we shall concentrate on general systems, which can be kept in the computer to assist with all types of program. These systems gain speed in two ways: one, by allowing the user to anticipate events and to give the system in advance instructions on how to proceed, rather than waiting for a human response time when the event occurs; and two, by making it possible to do two or more processes simultaneously. The first lies almost entirely in the realm of Operating Systems rather than Executive and here we pursue the second. Chiefly, the things that are worth doing in parallel are computing in the central processor and driving the various 'peripheral' devices.

The data for a computer has to get in and the results have to get out. Files that are only to be re-used by the machine must be output on to some medium and input again when required, since they cannot be economically held in fast store. The straightforward procedure is to read a record just before it is wanted and output the result completely as soon as it is produced. Unfortunately, of course, any job done in this way will take the sum of the times to read, the times to compute and those to output, and such are the relative disparities between reading an external medium and doing one internal operation that the total of the computing time for a record is (for most jobs) comparable to reading or writing time. Hence the hardware specifically required for any one of the operations spends much of its time idle. Moreover, little extra hardware needs adding to allow all three operations to proceed simultaneously. The record is transferred between the central processor and the peripheral either by adding fast buffer stores capable of containing a block of data to the peripherals or, more common nowadays, by 'stealing' a store cycle from the main store when the next word or character is ready for transfer. The mechanics need not here concern us further—the record is made available or removed without significant effect on the central processor speed.

Clearly now one simple way to take advantage of this is to read the next record (or block if several records are grouped for economy) while writing the last and processing the current one. But this will only give ideal results if the time for computing is the same as that for input and output for each block, an improbable situation. In general, we shall find some programs where the processing time is always less than the reading or writing time, others where it is always more, and a third class which alternate between the two, reading a batch of data, doing a lengthy process and then printing a batch of results. The third class may be able to be turned into one of the other two by dividing it into members, or by 'off-lining' as will be described later. We can now produce further economies by 'multiprogramming'.

2.4 Multiprogramming

By multiprogramming as explained in 1.2, we mean running two or more programs 'at once'; this does not mean that both programs are running at a given microsecond, but that the central processor switches from running one to another and back again, doing all the jobs together rather than running one program to completion. The object is to keep the central processor busy instead of having it idle while waiting for one program's peripheral transfers to finish.

Let us consider the two extreme cases of our programs in the previous section, one updating a file, with a few calculations but much reading and writing of magnetic tape, and the other, say performing calculations and only occasionally printing its results. Even with reading in advance the usage picture if we run one followed by the other is thus:

```
    CP              -  -  -  -   ___________
    MT              ___________
    LP                              __ __ __ __
                    Program 1    Program 2
```

Now suppose we could arrange to do the computing for the second in the gaps of the first:

```
    CP (doing 1)    -  -  -  -
    CP (doing 2)     __ __ __ __
    MT              ___________
    LP               __ __ __ __
```

We are running the first as fast as before, and the second at say nine-tenths of its normal speed. So if the time for each job was one hour the total time to do the two jobs would be only one hour six minutes instead of two hours. We can do this by holding both programs in store and running the first while it has anything to do; when it gets held up waiting for the tape deck, we switch to the second and when the tape transfer awaited is finished, we switch back to the first, and so on.

Of course, we have taken two ideal programs to run together, and in practice no installation would have just the right balance of central-processor limited and of peripheral-limited programs. However we gain as much by running together two peripheral-limited programs, interleaving their record processing, provided they do not require the same peripheral; an example might be a program copying cards to a magnetic tape and another reading another magnetic tape and printing from it. Note in this example that we can assume a tape system which does *not* allow simultaneous reading and writing; provided that reading and line printing time are much longer (as they normally would be here) than the tape reading or writing time, we shall in addition to making double use of our central processor also be doing the same for our tape system. We could add yet more peripheral limited programs, and then if there were still central processor time left over and we had a calculating program as well we could add that and run it when none of the peripheral limited program was running so that there were four, five or more programs apparently going on at the same time. Now the operation is, of course, only practical if our central processor is fast enough in terms of processing records, but in practice this is usual nowadays even with a smaller machine. Note also, incidentally, that in the first example, an alternative to doing the job in nearly half the time would be to get a processor half as slow, and still to do twice as much of the peripheral-limited work!

To do this, what have we paid? Well firstly we need the extra core store to hold the extra program. This may or may not be a real additional expense since it is rare for all programs to use the whole core, whose capacity is dictated by that of the largest program segment needed plus an amount to make this up to a standard size. Even if it is, doubling (say) the machine's capacity would generally justify the purchase of a little more core store. In practice, to do effective multiprogramming one must usually add more than just core store, since nearly all programs require some input and some output device; though as explained below this may be largely avoided if 'off-lining' is possible. Even without this, however, a factor of two or more in effective throughput over a shift may be attained in practice with a relatively small addition to the installation.

Multiprogramming of the type described here is generally carried out by having a control program which determines which of the programs to enter when. This program is one part of Executive.

2.5 'Off-lining'

'Off-lining' is properly a subject for a later chapter. We go into it here just enough to show its important relation to multiprogramming.

We have touched on two problems in the previous section which are, in fact, problems not of making the most effective use of our central processor, but of our input and output peripherals (e.g. card reader and line printer). First we have the program which required bursts of input followed later by bursts of output. Then there are the programs which only require input, or only print occasionally, but which we cannot multiprogram with other programs needing the same devices. If the system contains a disc (or a drum) we can solve this problem by reading the input to the disc in advance, calling the input from the disc as required, putting the results on to it, and then printing the results in a bunch later. Thus we do our input and output 'off-line' to the main program. The disc transfers, of course, should be done in blocks and take no significant time compared to the 'slow' peripheral transfers. In this way we free the two devices for the time of the main calculation so they can be used for other programs. Alternatively we may do all our card reading and line printing in this way, keeping two programs in the machine just to read card files to disc and to the output files. Ideally we can then run our two devices flat out, one reading the card data for a future program, the other printing data for a past program in parallel with running the current program whose data is already on the disc and which puts its results there. These programs form a perfect set for multiprogramming, especially since the transcribing programs are fairly small in their use of core store. Further multiprogramming of main programs may also be done to fill the time waiting for the disc, or other main file devices such as magnetic tape.

2.6 Subprogramming or tasking

A special form of multiprogramming is to multiprogram parts of one program together. The original program sets up members within itself which it wants driven autonomously so as to gain the benefits of multiprogramming between tasks within itself. There are a number of names for this process including 'subprogramming' and 'tasking'.

The use of this technique can be illustrated by two examples. First, consider the program which does bursts of input, then calculates, then does bursts of output. An alternative to off-lining the input and output by separate programs is in effect to do so within the existing one. This could be a more convenient approach if the volume was large but the amount produced after bursts of calculation was small enough to keep in the core store (or perhaps was produced fairly continuously during calculation but at an erratic rate). The output of the main program is put into a queue (in core let us suppose) and the member controlling output prints from the head of the queue. The inverse can be happening with another member controlling input. The three members (the main program being one) are multiprogrammed by the system exactly as if they were independent programs; they must, of course, contain interlocks between themselves to cope with situations when the queues become empty, or full.

The second illustration is given by considering a device which by its nature gives erratic rates of transfer, for example receiving messages from a number of manually operated typewriters. Here by controlling the device by a member program not only can we smooth out the flow of messages to the main program and also organise queues for each of the typewriters, but further this member can give any immediate replies required by the typewriters as soon as the transfer is complete. (The method may not be entirely clear until after the discussion of peripheral interrupts later.)

2.7 Multiaccess

A further form of parallel running is that mentioned in 1.2, Multiaccess. This is a main topic of a later chapter and so is only introduced here. Multiaccess derives from the wish to have a computer on tap to a human user. An individual user would for many purposes, including program check-out, like to start his program, run it for a time then sit and think, type in more data or alterations, run it a bit more and so on. But for one user to tie up the machine in this way is wasteful (though quite often done) even on a small machine and prohibitively expensive on a large one, since the human delays mean the processor spends most of its time standing idle. The solution is to multiprogram the programs of each of the large number of users. We give each user a console (say a typewriter) and we off-line any input and output not going to that. But we now find we have so many programs that the core store requirements are enormous. The solution to this is not to hold all the programs in store, but to swap them in and out from a drum or disc. In this way a multiprogramming effect is obtained, it is on a coarser timescale than that involved in switching between programs in store, but this is adequate in practical cases to give fast enough service to the human users.

This type of parallel operation is called Multiaccess, and differs from the multiprogramming previously discussed both in its technique, that of swapping programs to and from the core store, and also in its function: for unlike the latter it does not attempt better throughput of the system, not, that is, until one considers the whole system to include its human users.

2.8 Peripheral Interrupt System

So far we have considered the benefits of parallel operation without discussing how to control it. We want to be running a peripheral in parallel with computing and to be able to switch out of the current program when it stops. One reason we may want to switch out is to restart the program which was waiting for the transfer so that it can process the next record and keep the peripheral going. But even when only running one program there may be some critical activity to be done as soon as the transfer is finished, for example for a peripheral which we cannot instantly stop we may immediately need to start the next transfer, which has previously been prepared. Or on any peripheral where it is possible to form a queue of orders we just want to start the next order in the queue.

One way of doing this switching out is for any program being run to enter periodically a routine at a time convenient to itself which tests to see if any event has occurred. This can be a satisfactory solution if the program is closely associated with the events as in the real time situation discussed in Chapter 9, but it is generally at best a chore and at worst is quite impracticable—in general multi-programming how does one program 'know' how often it has to look for another program's events? A much more satisfactory way is to arrange that the peripheral sends a signal to the processor hardware on completion of the transfer and that the hardware on receipt of this signal interrupts the current program sequence, storing any registers it needs to free, and then enters a special program, which identifies the cause of the interrupt and decides what to do. The decision and resultant action is complex and will vary with the type of peripheral transfer; for this reason doing it by hardware would be expensive, would need peripheral dependent hardware in the central processor and would be dangerously inflexible. Hence, while considerable hardware assistance may be provided on a large machine, it is essentially, as stated, a software program, which is appropriate to this function.

This program is the nucleus of Executive.

3

FURTHER EXECUTIVE FACILITIES

BRIAN MILLIS

In Chapter 2 Brian Millis introduced the concept of Executive and discussed its multiprogramming role. Now he carries the story further by considering multiprogramming priorities, the allocation of core store and assignment of peripherals, and operator communication. Finally, after some discussion of its relationship with larger operating systems, he summarises by considering the profile of an Executive.

3.1 Development of Executives

We have now shown the need for a control program to deal with peripheral interrupts and organise multiprogramming. Historically this is why Executive programs came in to being and the rest of the story of their development tells first of the inclusion of further control to make multiprogramming practicable, second of the addition of facilities now more conveniently done in a central control program and third of applying the ideas on software given earlier.

Under the first head we may include multiprogramming priorities, program loading and core allocation, program protection, peripheral assignment and control, and control of operator communications, and processor error recovery. Under the second come peripheral error recovery, program chaining, logging, post-mortem aids and off-lining assistance. The application of the ideas on software affects the manner and extent to which these things are done.

3.2 Multiprogramming priorities

In the first example we had of multiprogramming there were two programs, one of which was peripheral limited and one central processor mill-time limited. The multiprogramming was done by using up the gaps in the mill-time use of the first to get on with the second. This is achieved by the first program informing Executive whenever it cannot proceed without getting another block of input or disposing of a block of output. Executive will suspend it (remembering why) and enter the second program. When the peripheral transfer is complete, it generates a signal resulting in the interruption of the second program and entry to Executive. Executive having identified the cause of the interruption can remove its reason for suspending the first program and re-enter this; obviously storing away the state of the second program, including its current order address, so it can be re-entered in due course at the point where it was interrupted. Executive will thus always re-enter the first program if it can be run; it will treat it as if it had higher priority for use of the central processor. If we multiprogram more peripheral-limited programs, clearly we must give all these higher 'priority' than the calculating program. But if at a given moment there is more than one peripheral-limited program to enter how do we select which one? If there are devices which require quick attention (and which Executive cannot itself deal with, for example by giving an already prepared and queued order) then we should give the relevant program priority; even if the interruption came in the middle of another program which, while peripheral limited, was dealing with a less critical device. Equally if one program, while often peripheral limited, was occasionally mill-time limited, it would clearly be sensible to give it a priority less than all the others but more than that of the purely calculating program. With the other programs in between it will often not matter very much which is given precedence; especially so if peripheral transfers are given one in advance and stored by Executive, as then it is unimportant when the program gets its mill time as long as it is given its fill once within every block transfer time. Thus one viable method of multiprogramming is to give every program a 'priority' which is roughly in proportion to the urgency with which it must respond to its peripherals and in inverse proportion to the amount of mill time used, and for Executive always to return central-processor control to the highest priority program which is currently able to run. We may note in passing that where a program both wants to use significant amounts of mill time and to respond quickly to some of its peripherals it may be possible to organise this by splitting the program into members as described in 2.6, 'Subprogramming or tasking'. Here each of the members which are multiprogrammed with each other has its own priority; the critical responses to the peripherals can thus be done by one high-priority member and the rest of the processing by a lower-priority one.

It must be emphasised that the priority system is purely a tool for allocating central processor time; the 'priorities' of the programs should be set so as to achieve best throughput of the system and do not correspond to any external priority of getting the job done. A program's priority may be set by assigning it a suitable number in the system's range on compilation; facilities will, however, usually be given to the operator or operating system to vary it to get better efficiency in a particular case. A program may also wish to vary its own priority, e.g. on changing from a calculating to a peripheral-limited phase. A sophisticated Executive might assign priorities by a learning technique, to get best throughput; with such an Executive external priorities for getting the jobs done might also be taken into account, but this would be in the context of allocation of all system resources.

There are simpler methods of allocating mill time. We could run each program in turn until it suspended itself waiting for a peripheral: as a method of multiprogramming several peripheral-limited programs without critical response times this is quite adequate and mill-limited programs could be added by making them give frequent dummy peripheral orders. Another method is to give each program a fixed amount of time (a 'time slice') in turn whenever it is able to run, this implies some sort of hardware 'clock' to initiate pulling out of the current program after the time has expired. Provided that the time can be kept sufficiently small this works adequately for many purposes though it does not allow very fast response to a critical peripheral. There are, however, problems in getting a small enough time without imposing excessive overheads due to frequent program changing. The ultimate in this scheme is to change programs on every instruction by hardware, having a set of hardware registers for each program. This has been done on one system, but the reliance on hardware switching and necessity for duplication would, in general, appear expensive and inflexible.

Allocating fixed time-slices does, unlike the priority system, allow several mill-time limited programs to be run together. But to do this is pointless in batch working since no greater throughput is achieved than by doing one followed by the other. Time-slice working, using coarse time slices relative to those above, is used for multiaccess systems but there, as we noted in an earlier section, the objective is not better throughput of the *machine*.

In practice, therefore, neither 'running to suspension' nor 'time-slice' gives as good a multiprogramming algorithm for general purposes as does the priority system; and the practical application of either in a general way is not as simple as might at first sight appear. However, they are sufficient for many purposes, and also they can be implemented on a machine without a peripheral interrupt system.

3.3 Program Loading, Core Management, etc

Once we have a system running under a multiprogramming Executive we must consider what happens when one program finishes and another is to be started. This needs to be done without disrupting the other programs being run, so Executive must either incorporate, or be able to call in, a program loader. But anyway how do we hold several programs in core? The simplest way would be to divide up the core store into several areas and specify that each program belongs to one area and can run nowhere else. This is unsatisfactory since we must at least allow programs to run in more than one place in store, and so the addresses written in the program before loading must be able to be converted into the 'absolute' core store position used. The most straightforward way to do this is to allocate to any one program a consecutive area of store, allow the program to be written assuming it starts at word 0 and then add to all core store addresses the distance from the start of the store ('absolute' word 0) to the position of its word 0, which is called its datum. This may be done by the loader, so that it is held in store with absolute address values, or it may be added dynamically by hardware when obeying the program. The latter; although it requires a special facility to be built into the hardware, has a number of advantages. First, in both systems one must only add the datum value to core addresses, not to literals, so in the former system core addresses must be distinguishable at load time. Second, if there are any address fields of limited extent, e.g. modifier addressed, which refer to core, there is no room to add the datum; which rules out the first scheme for machine designs where special treatment of these areas is impracticable. But most of all, in the latter system the program is held in core in a constant and relocatable form, hence any manipulation of core store addresses by the programmer (intentional or otherwise) will give a constant result; and it is possible, at any time when nothing is happening in the program for Executive to move it up or down the store. ('Nothing is happening' mainly means no peripherals are currently transferring to or from the program's area.)

This is an advantage for, if programs cannot be moved in store, the successor of a program must (in general) be loaded into precisely the space it vacated; in effect, therefore, the store has to be partioned for one session of running into a number of fixed length slots. But if the other programs can be moved, all free store can be amalgamated into a consecutive block and so the size of the various slots can change as required. Hence also the facility can be provided for a program to expand to make use of any free store available.

There are other solutions to the core allocation problem which do not require the program to be held in consecutive store. One is to have a machine architecture in which it is impossible to generate a core store address except as a displacement from a base address held in a table which is under the control of Executive. This allows the logically distinct areas of a program to be split up; but, as these are of variable size, amalgamation of freed areas; and hence movement of parts of a program still needs to be done. Another is to divide up the store into blocks, say (in a binary machine) of 1024 words each, to assign each program the number of blocks it needs without trying to keep these consecutive, and then dynamically by hardware to translate the part of the address given by the program into the actual block number assigned, by reference to a table built up on loading. To do this at a reasonable speed normally requires a significant amount of hardware, and is therefore a technique only applicable to larger machines. It is, however, a technique of some power as once the translation process exists it is possible to trap block addresses which have no corresponding address in core. This may be used to address blocks which need to be overlaid from backing store. Once again we have opened the door on to a large subject which we can pursue at this time no further—the name of this one is 'paging'.

But whatever system is used, there is a further important facility wanted. This is to be able to prevent one program from accidentally corrupting the Executive control program or any other multi-programmed with it. Theoretically, to guard against program errors is never an absolute requirement; it can be argued that the risk with well-tested programs is no more than that of, say, hardware failure, or again that with suitable higher-level languages and compilers the risk can be made negligible if not eliminated. But to rely on 'tested' programs is unwise and moreover removes the very useful ability to test new programs in parallel with running live work. The second argument is, of course, valid if we can ensure all programs are written in sufficiently high-level languages and the machine and compiler design is such as to make inter-program corruption impossible; this is one way of implementing protection and is used in at least one computing system. However, short of this, the consequences of one program causing mysterious errors in another are potentially so serious (to start with the diagnosis of what has happened is not easy) that some form of protection has been thought necessary in nearly every design for a multiprogramming computer.

Protection may be given by having a permission bit for each 'block' of store and setting these appropriately on program switching; the size of block being a compromise between the cost and overheads of many bits and keeping the units in which store can be allocated as small as possible. Or the blocks of store may be marked with the owning program's number, this being compared with the current program number on core access. This has on one system even been carried to the extent of marking each core word, having another four bits in it for this purpose.

When programs are allocated consecutive core store, the upper and lower bounds of the area may be held and all addresses compared (by hardware) with these before accessing the core store. If we are already adding the lower bound, the 'datum', this just requires the addition of comparison against a 'limit'. 'Datum-and-limit' can be extended to fragmented store by adding further registers and performing multiple comparison followed by the addition of the appropriate datum; but if the number of fragments gets above about four the cost and overheads in switching time compare unfavourably with other methods. Finally, protection comes naturally with address translation techniques such as paging, where invalid block addresses are recognised in attempting translation.

To prevent program corruption, it is sufficient to protect only against writing into foreign core store. This allows the programs to obey common code, to use common tables and to communicate with one another. But this is not always quite so simple as it seems due to the complications of address variation and program relocatability. It also implies a lack of privacy which may be objectionable for certain applications. Finally, though of less importance, accidental reading from a place which, being outside the program's area, may contain indeterminate information can produce program errors difficult to diagnose. Often, therefore, protection is absolute, no form of access to other areas being allowed. In more elaborate systems, to get the best of both worlds, different types of access permission may be introduced; thus three permission bits may be held for each block controlling operand reading, writing and obeying code. In the paging scheme the problems of inter program addressing may be solved by translating (possibly different) block addresses in different programs to the same absolute address; thus for example we could here have one program updating a table as its block address 3, while another had read-only access to it as its block address 7.

3.4 Peripheral Assignment and Control, Operator Communication

For similar reasons to those which require Executive to control the use of core store between programs and to handle the timesharing, it must also do the same for peripherals. It is clearly desirable that a program which requires, say, four magnetic tape decks on an installation with eight should be able to use any four of the eight. It is also desirable to prevent it interfering with another program by using its peripherals accidentally. This is most simply done by letting the program address its decks by 'logical' numbers, say 0, 1, 2, 3, and having Executive translate these to the physical addresses of the decks which have been allocated to correspond to these logical numbers for the current run of the program. (It is possible to do the translation by program rather than hardware since instantaneous speed is not necessary.)

The most elementary way of allocating physical units to the logical numbers would for Executive on coming across the first mention of any number to allocate to it arbitrarily any device of that kind that was currently unused. This is a possible method for allocation of card readers, line printers, etc, on an installation with not more than two or three of each kind. However, even here it is preferable to have a separate 'allocation request' order given by the program to Executive before using the device. This allows the allocation to be done more easily in a preliminary part of the program, Executive can inform the program at this point if no such device is available, or of any peculiar details about the particular one allocated. Program-error protection is improved since any mention of an unallocated number other than by this order can be trapped as a fault. But moreover all special requirements for the device (e.g. that a line printer with 120 print positions is required on an installation with several different printers) can be specified as part of this order and do not need to be tied to normal transfer orders. This can be extended so these last orders do not even have to indicate the type of device, they use a logical device number only, the 'allocate' order having specified that this was to be a card-reader or whatever.

An alternative to specification by 'allocate' order in the program, is to give the device requirements as information accompanying the program when loaded. While this does have the advantage that a program whose peripheral demands cannot currently be satisfied can be rejected before being loaded, it is less flexible in other ways. A program may be able to run without a peripheral (e.g. a second line printer in some cases), or more likely, it may be able to use a substitute after some modification to itself. Also it is undesirable to have to allocate, say, a card punch at the start of a long program run, if this is only required to punch some results at the end. For these reasons, allocation on loading will generally only be provided as an optional alternative to an allocate order.

However, any system where allocation is done by arbitrary choice from the pool of free units is not satisfactory for tape-deck allocation. Here it is almost essential to be allowed to load tapes at will before they are allocated, particularly if a tape is already there as the result of a previous run. This is done by having the first block on the tape a header label in some standard format, containing a name (this is, of course, desirable for checking purposes anyway). The program allocate order for tapes is then extended to include a name and on receiving this Executive will search the unallocated decks reading the labels looking for one which matches the requested name; it will allocate the corresponding deck if successful, otherwise inform the program, or suspend the program and request the operator to load a tape with this name. If a tape is to receive output only, it still needs a label, so it can be searched; the program may call for a specific tape to hold its output, or in some systems it may call for any of a pool of available tapes, these might be identified by having a retention date in the label and using for output any tape whose retention date had expired. In the latter case at least, the program would want to write its own label on the allocated tape and it is convenient to combine this with allocation and have Executive do it. The above process of allocation by naming the required file is known as 'opening' the file.

The tape-allocation scheme may also be applied to other input devices. It should be noted, however, that unless it is possible to backspace over the header block this has to be held by Executive, this may be desirable to save re-reading anyway, but it is then essential that Executive is informed by a recognisable interrupt if the reel is changed by the operator.

In all cases where allocation is other than by recognition of a document or file name, some method of allowing the operator to force the allocation of a particular device should be provided. This is even true for output devices, on a line printer it is possible to identify the source by printing a front sheet, but if preprinted stationery is required, and the system arbitrarily chooses the line printer to be used, at best time will be lost while the operator staggers over with the paper and loads it.

In going on to consider Direct Access devices we meet another requirement. We must clearly allow the several programs in the machine to share the use of a large fixed disc or drum. With exchangeable disc systems it is possible to treat the disc cartridges like tapes and to assign the whole cartridge and the handler it is on to one program. However, even here one would like to make use of the direct access nature of the device to allow several concurrently running programs each to keep their smaller files and working areas on a common cartridge. If this is done there are problems as to when the cartridge can be changed and so this sharing should, in general, be confined to those handlers which can be used as fixed discs for the run. The sharing can extend to programs having common access to parts of the disc or drum, particularly useful for system data and library subroutines, it can also be used for communication between programs. In many ways, this commonly accessible area resembles core store, especially when used as work space, and the allocation and protection problems are the same. In some schemes Executive controls the space in a similar way, allocating blocks as required, indeed the space may be treated as an extension of core store and once again we are nearing the door of 'paging'.

But especially for permanent data it is more usual to present them as files which may be accessed in a 'direct' (e.g. random or indexed) manner. In this case Executive must control the access by taking the block or track address (as appropriate) in the file which is given by the program and converting to the absolute address on the disc. Once this mechanism exists, it may be used within one program to refer to different areas on the same disc by different file names, which is very convenient both conceptually and to avoid problems if the 'files' need to be moved within the disc area, or to be split between different exchangeable disc cartridges later. These facilities and those of tape seeking and labelling, with the 'logical' to 'physical' conversions of unit numbers and file addresses are a considerable help even on a system just running one program at a time.

The system may only permit files to occupy consecutive area on the disc, in this case the process of address conversion is simply to add a datum appropriate to the file to it. More elaborate layouts are also possible. The position of the files may be entirely under Executive control, so that it may shuffle them round to make room for others if desirable, or the areas may be set up only when the file is initiated. The latter is more appropriate for large files on devices using moving heads, as the characteristics of the file layout and the program using it can be then dovetailed to minimise head movement.

We now go on to Operator Communications. The operator and his console represent a peripheral which needs to be shared amongst the various programs. One solution is to have several consoles and allocate one to each program, rather like peripherals except that the console can specify the program to be loaded, rather than the program allocating itself a console. But this is clearly unnecessary and if the console is a typewriter (as most are currently) it is sufficient to type the program identity before output messages and for the operator to type it in input messages. This provides an adequate means for controlling three or four program streams; it would become confusing for a larger number, but then one would expect to be using a powerful Operating System. Executive must determine the program referred to in input messages and should add the program identity to output messages. In addition Executive will generate messages itself, these will depend on the system, but might for example include indications of detected program error, or which peripheral had been allocated to a program. The operator will need to supply messages to Executive, for example about what program is to be loaded next. Thus Executive is involved in a considerable amount of typewriter control and interpretation of messages.

3.5 Executives and Operating Systems

To complete the picture of Executive we must discuss the differences, and the overlap, between it and an Operating System. We have seen how the pursuit of parallel operation leads to having a central control program, Executive. We mentioned that another approach to greater efficiency is to reduce the need for operator intervention, and this implies giving the system advance instructions on how to proceed, and having a control program to take the appropriate actions on program events. This control program is naturally extended to assist with resource allocation, advance input of data (off-lining), and forms the nucleus of what has become called an 'Operating System'.

Historically, these paths to a central control program have been followed side by side, with greater or less emphasis being placed on either aspect by different people. But by whatever route, master control programs have been evolved and have been variously called Executive, Master Program, Supervisor or Operating System. The term Operating System is broader than the others: it usually includes ancillary routines such as, for example, the off line input-output routines and can embrace the compilers associated with the system.

Within a system it is sometimes useful to distinguish between an inner 'Executive' and an outer 'Operating System'. In a medium-to-large system, there will be a complex control program which in practice has to be split up somehow. One reasonable separation is between the necessarily fast microscopic control of parallel operation with program changes at millisecond rates, which must for speed be core resident, and the longer term macroscopic control of which program is to be called into the machine next, which need not. The microscopic control can form an inner section, which enters the outer control when it traps relevant events in the programs. We may call this inner section the Executive of the system. It will control the multiprogramming between programs in core store, the giving of peripheral transfers and the handling of the interrupts. Such things as operator communication, peripheral allocation, detected program errors or time-out, will be left to (or passed to) the outer system to deal with.

This distinction is purely one of implementation; there is no *a priori* split between the functions of the Executive part and that of the Outer Operating System, though the latter part will tend to do the more macroscopic Operating System control functions. The position of the boundary will vary from system to system and should be chosen solely for efficiency and ease of organisation. But unfortunately this, and the elastic extent of the Operating System (e.g. in regard to inclusion of compilers) means that comparison of the Executive or Supervisor and Operating System of one computer with those of another must be done with care.

Other distinctions may be made in a system with more than one level of control. We have discussed in a previous section the possible reasons for this type of system; where a base Supervisor or Executive is in control of the whole system, but one of the programs under its control is itself a control program running its own object programs. As has been said, this may be done to provide extra or specialised Operating System functions and thus we have free standing Operating Systems distinct from the Executive.

We have, therefore, a distinction between the Operating System approach to a central control program and that of a parallel processing Executive; and we have a distinction in a particular system between an 'Executive' and an 'Operating System'. But the implementation split where it exists is a pragmatic one made for purely practical considerations and will at most roughly follow any functional distinction. On a small-to-medium system an integrated central program will almost certainly be desirable for efficiency; and any free-standing Executive able to run object programs by itself must contain some 'Operating System' type facilities to work.

3.6 Profile of an Executive

To illustrate what has been said so far, we now present a profile by functions of an Executive. An Executive which performed all the functions listed might be appropriate to a system slightly larger than the minimum capable of supporting multiprogramming. Such a system would be likely to have some facilities for control by 'job description' as described in Chapter 4, here we just indicate the areas where this might affect the other functions performed. Similarly program swapping for multiaccess might be done on this system if it included suitable console devices, probably in a restricted way.

1. *Internal functions*

   Provision of commonly required internal (i.e. Central Processor type) functions which are not performed by hardware on this computer. Entered by Extracode. Provision of such functions may be to get range compatibility of Central Processor.

2. *Peripheral control*

   Checks validity of object program's instructions. Translates 'Logical' unit numbers and addresses to 'physical' ones. Looks after intimate peripheral control (timing and sequence of control commands). Decodes peripheral interrupts, obtains peripheral status and performs any appropriate error recovery/error monitoring; gives results to and if appropriate desuspends object program. Controls queuing of orders, and disc head movement optimisation, etc. Provides macros to program in terms of hardware commands (e.g. separate head movement and transfer can be carried out as a result of one object program instruction). Can arrange for compatibility to object program of peripherals of the same class but with different hardware facilities.

3. *Multiprogramming*

   Controls allocation of mill time between object programs. In a priority based scheme, suspends programs when unable to proceed (waiting for peripheral transfer, operator action, another program's or subprogram's action, etc) and desuspends as appropriate; always re-enters highest priority unsuspended program. Allows multiprogramming between parts of the same program. Possibly swaps programs out of core in multiaccess system. Multiprograms system actions with object programs. May revise priorities for mill-time usage. Allows programs to be written independently of each other. Protects against program interference with another, or with Executive by setting hardware controls and/or checking transfer bounds by software. Provides for legitimate inter-program communication. Allocates resources.

4. *Core Store management*

Allocates core store to programs. Provides for relativising/translating of addresses (in conjunction with hardware); and hence program independence of absolute position in store. Relocates programs within core store as necessary. Controls 'paging' (where provided).

5. *Peripheral assignment*

Assigns peripherals to programs (setting up logical to physical unit ties), according physical requirements and/or labels. Divides multi-mechanism peripherals between programs; also divides areas of Direct Access store. Maintains file directories and labels.

6. *Off-lining*

Re-directs peripheral transfers for 'off-line' peripherals. Multiprograms any off-line input or output program with other work. (See Chapters 4 and 5 for further details of off-line control.)

7. *Fault detection*

Traps any illegal instructions in object programs and takes monitoring action (possibly according to job description). Traps some hardware errors, e.g. core store parity failure, providing information for engineer and keeping unaffected programs running (see also 'peripheral control' for errors there).

8. *Logging*

Provides a log of activities, possibly on console typewriter, possibly on disc file, etc, from which information for system performance statistics (including device error rates) and/or accounting.

9. *Program loading, chaining, etc*

Loads programs, will find the requested one from a file of programs. Calls in successor program as nominated by program, or under control of a message stream or job description.

10. *Operator communications*

Controls communications from object program to operator and conversely; may substitute automatic action as directed by job description if relevant. Communicates to operator state of the system for information and directives (e.g. to load a tape) requiring operator action. Receives from operator directives about which programs to run, which peripherals to assign, etc.

11. *Miscellaneous*

Provides to operator facilities, e.g. for printing contents of parts of core store, for dumping programs. Provides to program facilities, e.g. for getting the time and date, for getting information about facilities available on the system and about itself (e.g. size of its allocated core store, physical numbers of its peripherals).

4

OPERATING SYSTEMS: INTRODUCTION TO GEORGE 1 AND GEORGE 2

PETER BURKINSHAW

Moving on from the basic facilities of Executive, Peter Burkinshaw introduces some concepts designed to reduce the involvement of the human operator. He elaborates some of the objectives and historical background introduced in Chapter 1, and explains the important principle of a Job Description, illustrating this by George 1. Next he discusses the concepts of Macros and off-lining in greater depth, and finally describes how George 2 is used to provide off-lining facilities.

4.1 Introduction

In recent years an Operating System has come to be regarded by most computer users as an essential part of their environment, particularly in the larger and more complex installations. Such operating systems represent a compromise between two, sometimes conflicting, goals:

1. *Improving the efficiency of use of the machine's resources by:*
   - (a) minimisation of set-up time between jobs.
   - (b) maximisation of the throughput of peripherals, ensuring, for example, high information densities per unit transfer (in engineering terms, 'increasing the signal to noise ratio'), and that the operating speed of the devices is as near as possible to the rated maximum, by what may be generally called sympathetic programming.
   - (c) maximisation of the number of arithmetic operations performed per unit time by, for example, suitable buffering of peripheral transfers, or even the disconnection of I/O devices from the program at execution time entirely.
   - (d) allowing for as many simultaneous users as possible in multi-access systems.
   - (e) minimisation of the turnaround time for 'short' jobs relative to long jobs.
   - (f) minimisation of the skill required to use the system.

2. *Improving the security of use of the machine, in the sense of ensuring that it has performed a task correctly rather than the degree of secrecy concerned, by:*
   (a) Good interface communications
   (b) Good control information
   (c) Diagnostic information
   (d) The provision of standards
   (e) The enforcement of standards where appropriate.

Clearly, to ensure that a job is done correctly, some statement of the job is necessary. This requires an interface between the man wanting the job done and the man sitting at the console 'pressing the buttons'. The interface could be outside the context of an operating system, but only at a price in terms both of efficiency and security which many would consider unreasonable. Where a statement of the job is in a coded form, that can be read and acted upon by an operating system, we call it a 'job description'. If anything goes wrong during the execution of a job and is detected by the operating system, it must be reported at the interface. To enhance efficiency, it is usually necessary to reduce the freedom of the programmer or user in some directions. This may appear to be more restrictive than it really is, for the imposition of standards can be beneficial, it can provide portmanteau facilities from which all can benefit, and which many would otherwise have to provide for themselves. But it is as well to remember that imposed standards must take account of the variety of jobs to be run, and that a flexible operating system must be fairly permissive.

4.2 Historical growth of operating system standards

The concept of a job description is, in fact, only the last step in a process of standards for operating procedures that has gone on for a long time. To appreciate this let us consider the developments that have taken place in the machine room by imagining ourselves back in the days when computers have just been invented, and no software of any kind yet exists. We have a machine with a card reader, card punch and line printer, and a central processing unit consisting of a control console, arithmetic, control and storage units. Let us attempt to enumerate the problems we may encounter in using this hardware, how we shall try to solve them, and what may happen if we don't.

The first thing we must do, if it is a question of wiring control panels or plugboards, is to establish input-output formats. For example we must specify a format for card input containing program instructions. If we do not, everyone will invent one for himself and we shall need a large number of control panels, between one per programmer and one per program written, depending on how often each programmer redesigns his program format before arriving at a satisfactory standard. This is clearly undesirable because much time and effort will be spent by each programmer duplicating the work of other programmers, the machine room area will become cluttered with control panels, the machine will be standing idle for longer and longer periods while the operator finds the correct panel, and an increasing number of jobs will be attempted with the wrong panel.

So we establish a standard format for programs on cards and a standard control panel to read them. Thinking along the same lines, we also standardise formats for data input on cards and output to printer. Such standardisation is an important part of an operating system.

The next thing we notice is how long it takes to load a program. It may take several minutes if there is only one machine instruction on each card. When programs were only a few hundred instructions long this format was acceptable, but now that they may contain thousands of instructions the time taken to load them is excessive. Until now the necessary loading orders have been on the same card as the instruction to be loaded, except for the initial read-order, keyed-in via the console. It would be better to have a program resident in store for the duration of loading which could handle program cards containing more than one instruction, and so we write a loader-routine which resides in a reserved area of store during the loading process. This means, of course, that no program using this standard 'loader' can contain instructions that will be assigned to the reserved area, but the area can be used by the program being loaded for the storage of variables generated during its execution.

We have made the loading process faster, we must now make it more efficient. We have noticed that the first or last cards of a program have an annoying habit of getting lost, or worse, turning up a week later at the wrong end of another program, thereby spoiling two program runs. So while we have the loader-routine in store, it might as well check identification, sequence and card count fields, as it loads. We make it do this and so achieve some of the other objectives defined earlier as those of an operating system.

Another thing we find—to our amazement—is that our programs don't always work first time, however short they are. This would force us to spend hours of our time, and the computer's, reading out words of store one at a time and comparing them with what we expect, if we didn't have a store print routine or dump-to-cards routine which allows us to postmortem programs at our desks. As it happens, the routine which does this more or less fits into the same amount of store as the loader routine. Since they are never required at the same time, they can occupy the same locations, and we load each as required. This implies that we cannot use the loading space at all now, but it was only available for restricted use before, so it is not greatly missed.

At first we operated our own programs, which seems natural while testing but became a chore after the program was fully tested and someone else wanted to use it. Unfortunately only the programmer who wrote it seems to know how to run it. How will anyone else know that when the program stops with a particular display, it means load another set of data into the reader and restart at some other point? What we must do is standardise the displays so that an *operator* can recognise them. The operator may not know how to write programs, so at first there is a communication problem. For example the operator doesn't know where to enter a program after loading. We solve that by enhancing the loader routine to accept another kind of card which says 'don't *load* this, but *do* it,' and we put on this card, which is the last in the program, an instruction saying 'branch to entry point'. Another thing the operator may not recognise is the display that means 'Please load the deck of cards which has in columns 47–53 the alphabetic equivalent of this two-digit display 'XXXXXXXX'. If, however, we prepare a standard data header card, possibly called a document header, and place it at the front of the data pack the loading-and-entering routine will be able to check the identity of the first data card and prevent a spoilt run. Our loading-and-entering routine is now doing a multitude of tasks, all geared to the accurate and efficient execution of programs; it is in fact part of our operating system.

We move on several years and re-examine the situation. The equipment now includes several magnetic tape units, a drum or disc unit, and a bigger and faster memory store. On the operational side, programs are being loaded from disc, drum, or magnetic tape, as well as cards or paper tape. Our primitive loader routine has been replaced by a core-resident Executive which includes our original loader routine, converses with the operator, sends messages to the user via the line printers, and produces messages for various other users such as the tape-library, accountants, work control and maintenance engineers. It embodies standards built up over the years, it obeys, informs and commands, permitting jobs prepared according to the rules of the system to be run, and rejecting others.

4.3 Job Descriptions

A job is, simply, all the things a user wishes to do at one time, for example, compile his source program, load and enter the resulting object program, allow it to read a set of data and when it has terminated, print out the contents of part of the store. It is clearly essential to make a statement of the required operations if they are not to be executed by the user himself. In the past either the operator knew how to run the job, or he was verbally briefed for a short job, or he was given a written brief for a longer, more complex, job, or he was given a stylised form, filled in by the user, with explanatory notes as necessary. On operating systems the way of conveying this information is a list of statements prepared according to the rules of a *job description language* defined in the manual. This list of statements is called a 'job description', and is usually encoded into cards or paper tape. It is read into the computer, and its instructions carried out, by the Operating System. In essence it is a program for a machine whose basic instruction set consist of such things as 'load program X into store', 'enter the currently loaded program at location Y', 'dump the currently loaded program onto device Z', etc., instead of a normal arithmetic instruction set. The following is an example of a Job description to carry out a compile-and-run FORTRAN Job:

Job Description	*Meaning*
`JOB FORTRAN, 77101, PBR`	name of job, A/C no., user's name
`IN MT (PROGRAM TAPE)`	open input library tape, load
`LOAD #XFAM`	FORTRAN compiler #XFAM from this tape
`IN /0 (SOURCE)`	the input FORTRAN program is on the same medium—cards—as the Job Description
`ENTER 1`	compiler entry point
`AT DELETED LO, GO TO 8`	if compilation succeeds, go to label 8 in Job description, otherwise—
`END`	end job, proceed to next job
`8 LOAD #`	load object program
`IN /0 (DATA)`	input data for the program is also on cards
`ENTER`	enter object program at standard entry point
`AT HALTED EP, END` `AT DELETED 00, END` }	end job when completed, or halted with display EP
`AT OTHER HALTED, ENTER 9`	in case of other halts, recovery/reentry point is 9.
`PRINT 0 TO 3000`	In case of all other events, e.g. program goes illegal, print locations 0 to 3000.
`****`	End Marker

4.4 GEORGE1

The Job Description used in this example was written for GEORGE 1, which was designed primarily to replace hand-operated Executive, on the larger and faster machines in the middle of the 1900 range. It had been noticed fairly early in the development of programs for 1904 and 1905 machines that jobs of fairly short duration, as many test runs are, were making extremely poor use of the computer, even with the most skilled operators. Another problem was that of getting complex jobs run correctly, because with a manually operated Executive the user either had to operate his own programs or write a statement of what he required done for a human operator to interpret, and the more complex a job was, the more susceptible this was to misinterpretation.

The operating system known as GEORGE 1 was designed to overcome these problems, but it also had to be capable of running all existing programs and jobs working in Executive environments. It became clear during the design phase that some features of 1900 Executive, designed in the early days of the machine series, were undesirable in the light of more recent developments. This was most noticeable in the areas of operator communication, magnetic tape security in a multiprogramming environment, and a certain lack of control of peripheral allocation, due to the design of the dynamic allocation system. What had to be produced was an Operating System which could be 'tacked-on' to Executive, supplementing its operation to make it handle jobs automatically, instead of handle programs manually. It also had to reduce the traffic jam of console messages, and override certain Executive actions inappropriate to the more advanced approach of an Operating System. Because GEORGE 1 had to be phased in to replace Executive many features of the system had to be optional: if it was inconvenient to use them, they could be by-passed and the program behaved as it would under Executive. For this reason, all Data declarations are optional with GEORGE 1, and no Document or Label checking will be done unless desired.

One area of job control which received special attention was allowing the anticipation of various unusual conditions which might arise either with programs under test, or proven programs. Previous systems based firmly in the 'control-card' era were not considered flexible enough. What was needed was a comprehensive set of conditional branches, capable of carrying control backwards or forwards within the job description. These were defined as the GEORGE 1 'AT list', in which any event could be selected for particular attention, just as a human operator might be directed to attend to such an event, but with the advantage that no depth of nesting of conditions and re-activation was too complex to be defined in the job description language.

The main features of GEORGE 1 are therefore:

1. that is is automatic in that encoded instructions are passed directly by the user to the system, with no human interpretation,

2. that it is possible, optionally, to check that a program's peripherals are loaded with the correct data by means of Document Headers and Tape Labels,
3. that the problems of duplicate Tape Labels may be overcome by allowing further resolution by Tape Serial Number, a physical and external identification which the operator can verify, as opposed to file-names which he can not,
4. that it is possible to override the file-names used in the control areas of a program, by means of declarations in the job description, and inform the program appropriately.
5. that a tape may be allocated merely by ALLOTing it and declaring the required tape only in the job description.
6. that it is possible to state what action is to be taken at any event which occurs during the execution of a program.
7. that operator intervention is restricted to physical actions such as loading peripherals.
8. that there is continuity of allocation of peripherals across program boundaries.

The area permanently required by GEORGE 1 (about 2000 24-bit words) is such that it is suitable for small machines with 16000 words of core store. As the system does not maximise the efficiency of peripheral use, apart from the greater security it offers, it was considered reasonable to allow continued access by the user to the program slots available in the environment of a multi-programming Executive, apart from the slot or slots in use by GEORGE 1 and the program under its control. In sections 4.6 and 4.7 we shall explore alternative systems designed to overcome the low efficiencies caused by imbalance of peripheral usage.

4.5 Macros

One of the simultaneous strengths and weaknesses of the human operator is his ability to learn, adapt, and apply his knowledge to new, but similar situations. It is obviously useful to be able to say to an operator 'You now face situation X', and for him to recognise it, and execute a complex sequence of operations. On the other hand, the dangers of an operator thinking 'I recognise this to be situation X', without being told so explicitly, grow rapidly the more he comes into contact with situations similar to, but not the same as X. The difficulty is that we cannot control the mask he applies in his subconscious pattern-recognition process of perceiving situation X. It is also hard for the operator to break free from his conditioning when although he is in situation X, a different response is required. Many programmers have experienced the hazards of developing a new version of a well-established and oft-used package in a manual operating system environment. The moment he sees it, the operator says ‘Ah, this is program Y, I know all about program Y because I’ve run it so often’. Unfortunately the situation this time is different, and almost without realising it he does the ‘right’ thing which happens to be wrong on this occasion. What the operator has developed is essentially a *macro-procedure*, or *macro*.

Most modern Operating Systems allow the user to build up a library of macros by means of programs which form part of the system and permit the creation and updating of files of such macros, which are usually kept on the same device or unit as the system itself. Operating System macros are usually of a type which is expanded into a set of primitive commands, and written so that various parametric fields are replaced by character-string substitutes in a calling sequence. The provision of macros has obvious benefits in the economy of labour required to use the system. A less obvious benefit is, that while all can enjoy the benefits of a macro-library, it in no way jeopardises one’s right not to use it; instead one can write out in longhand anything that cannot be expressed by the macro. This is obviously more flexible than using a manual system in which operating habits develop which are difficult to by-pass. The provision of macro facilities is one of the features of the enhanced GEORGE 1 system known as GEORGE 2.

The following is an example of a GEORGE 2 system macro for Compile-and-run FORTRAN:

	Meaning
`MACDEF FORTRUN`	definition of macro ‘Fortrun’ follows
`IN MT(PROGRAM TAPE)`	open input library tape
`LOAD #XFAM`	load FORTRAN compiler #XFAM from this tape
`IN %A`	input source program—name and medium
`ENTER %B`	compiler entry point

`9FR1 AT HALTED EC, GO TO 9FR2`
`AT DELETED LO, GO TO 9FR4`
`AT HALTED SM, GO TO %C`
`AT HALTED CE, ENTER 6`
`AT HALTED ST, GO TO 9FR3`
`AT HALTED LD, RESUME`
`AT FAIL, GO TO %D`
	label 9FR1—
	‘AT’ list: action to be taken at specified events, i.e. halts during or at end of compilation

`9FR3 HALT 'NEEDS CORE'` `RESUME, 9FR1`	*label 9FR3:* resume compilation at 9FR1 after more store has been given by operator.
`9FR2 IN MT (PROGRAM %E)`	*label 9FR2:* the object program is on mag. tape labelled per parameter
`LOAD #%E`	load object program

`GO TO 9FR5`	go to label 9FR5
`9FR4 LOAD #`	*label 9FR4:* load object program whose name and medium were quoted in last DELETED message
`9FR5 IN %F`	*label 9FR5:* input data for object program (name and medium)
`ENTER %G`	object program entry point
`ENDMAC FORTRUN`	end of macro definition

The macro call line for this FORTRUN macro will take the form

```
FORTRUN %A, %B, %C, %D, %E, %F, %G
```

When such a macro call line is encountered, GEORGE will replace it by the stored macro definition, substituting for the parameters %A to %G:

%A— program description document
%B— entry point to #XFAM
%C— label to transfer to if there are missing segments
%D— label to transfer to if the compilation fails
%E— name of compiled program
%F— input data for the compiled program
%G— entry point to the compiled program.

Thus, assuming the job description is on cards, to compile the non-overlaid FORTRAN program #TRAN held on cards and run it, entering at entry point 7, when its data will be read from paper tape, the parameters will be set as follows:

`%A=/0(SOURCE)`	—card input to #XFAM
`%B=1`	—entry point for #XFAM
`%C=6`	—label elsewhere in job description
`%D=7`	—label elsewhere in job description
`%E=TRAN`	—name of compiled program
`%F=TRO (DATA)`	—tape input to #TRAN
`%G=7`	—entry point for #TRAN

Thus, all that need be written as a job description is:

```
   JOB COMPILETRAN, 77777, THE USER
   FORTRUN /0(SOURCE), 1, 6, 7, TRAN, TRO(DATA), 7
   AT HALTED OK, END
   AT FAIL, GO TO 8
6  DISPLAY 'SEGMENTS MISSING'
   ENDJOB
7  DISPLAY 'COMPILATION FAILURE'
   ENDJOB
8  PRINT O(100)
   ****
```

4.6 Peripheral inefficiency

All normal conventional programs process input, in the form of punched cards or paper tape, and produce output either on the same media or on a line printer, or both. They may also process files of data on magnetic backing stores. Such programs form a spectrum defined by the degree to which their execution is limited by their input-output requirements. They range from the traditional 'commercial data processing' programs to 'scientific' or 'number-crunching' programs. The first type spends most of its time waiting for the execution of input-output instructions and the power of the processor, or mill, is largely wasted. The second type spends most of its time performing arithmetic, and only rarely needs to read, or print results. Clearly no absolute division exists between the two types, as a given job will appear under different guises according to the configuration on which the job is run. Thus with an infinitely fast processor, all jobs would appear to be of a data-processing type, whereas with infinitely fast peripherals, all jobs would appear to be of the 'number-crunching' type. For a given configuration only one kind of job can achieve optimum performance and that is the job which performs its input-output operations at the exact frequency which is the rated maximum for the equipment. Given the most sympathetic programming, the probability of an installation meeting even one such perfect job is very small. The depressing truth is that about as much processor time will be wasted waiting for the 'principal' input-output devices of the configuration to act, as they in turn waste idling at other times, considering the work load of the installation as a whole. The degree of waste is dependant on the deviation of the jobs from the optimum. The greater the diversity of jobs, the more time will be unavoidably lost.

Or is it really unavoidable? A partial solution is to employ multiprogramming techniques to offset wasted time in the execution of jobs which have a profile from the opposite end of the spectrum, and whose peripheral requirements do not clash. But it is unlikely that users will be eager to purchase more card input-output equipment or more printers than they theoretically need, though most users of computers need to have their results printed, regardless of volume. This clash can lead to pressure on the writers of programs making little use of the printer, to give it up entirely, and substitute, for example, console typewriter output. If such programs can be detected sufficiently early in their gestation, it may be possible to persuade their writers to do this. Unfortunately, even programs which eventually turn out to have little output will go through phases of compilation and testing which require large volumes of printing. Thus, early in the life of any program, it exhibits 'data-processing' type characteristics.

4.7 Off-lining

There is an alternative solution to the problem of waste peripheral and processor time when sufficient spare resources of backing store and core store can be diverted for the purpose. This alternative is to *off-line* the input-output of the job. By this is meant to transfer the input of the job to backing store prior to the job's execution and to transfer the output from backing store to the appropriate device subsequent to the execution of the job. During execution of the job, depending on the design of the system, it need not be apparent to programs whether or not they are reading their input from, or writing their output to, the device ultimately intended. The actual reading, or printing or punching, takes place completely independently, under control of separate programs, which may even be run on separate machines from the main body of the job. These are the principles of off-line processing. The main advantages it offers are:

1. It smooths out variations in demand for peripheral activity in a way unattainable by multiprogramming alone.
2. As the backing store medium used as an intermediary is magnetic rather than mechanical, the transcription time, at the object program interface, is minimised, and during the real input or output phases, the peripherals are driven at maximum speed.
3. It may be advantageous from the core-store scheduling point of view, because the object programs, which are generally much larger than the transcription programs, may run faster.

There are other, less tangible gains in the security and other aspects of the system:

4. Peripherals tend to perform better when working at uniform rates, rather than irregularly.
5. Jobs naturally break down into three phases: input, process and output. A breakdown in any phase only necessitates re-running from that phase on. Similarly if duplicate copies of output are required they can be retrieved cheaply, if requested within a finite period after the job is complete.

Against these advantages one must set the following direct and indirect costs:

1. The off-line routines require core store and file devices, such as magnetic tape decks, or disk space, on the same computer: or a satellite computer.
2. If used on the same computer ('*pseudo-off-lining*') the routines may well aggravate the channel scheduling problems on the channels of the off-line devices.
3. Sequence and other input errors may not be trapped before processing proper. If this is sufficiently serious, it may be

necessary to write special transcription routines for important large-volume files, incorporating special validation not normally available in the standard package.

4. The increased complexity will result in uncertainty if errors arise, unless special checks are devised at each phase to ensure the highest standards of data reliability.
5. Inevitably, it will be impossible to operate some jobs in an off-line manner: for example, any job requiring two phased input streams, such as the comparison of two paper tapes. Other jobs, such as the diagnostic print of a magnetic tape may not benefit from it.
6. No program can be run in an off-line manner if it utilises any facilities, which may be provided by the hardware, to send information dynamically to input devices, such as the various modes of reading paper tape, or if it makes use of dynamic information from output devices in any way which cannot be standardised, for example, page overflow or paper low on printers.

4.8 GEORGE 2

The 1900 Operating System GEORGE 2 was designed as an enhanced version of GEORGE 1, with macro facilities as described in 4.5 and with off-line peripheral processing. The off-line facilities can be used in such a way that:

(a) input and output are off-lined
(b) output only is off-lined
(c) neither input nor output is off-lined, i.e. as in GEORGE 1.

GEORGE 2 is available in two variants. One is resident on magnetic tape and provides off-line facilities via magnetic tape, the other is resident on disc (or drum) and provides a choice of off-line media between magnetic tape or disc.

GEORGE 2 really consists of three distinct programs, the off-line card or paper tape to magnetic medium transcription program, the off-line magnetic medium to card or paper tape punch, or line printer program, and a central module. The most effective means of using the system is to use all three parts at the same time. Thus at a given point, job-batch A will be processed by the output program while batch B is being run, and batch C is being created by the input routine. This necessitates the use of up to four program slots, dependent on the Executive and version of the system in use.

Because of its extra facilities GEORGE 2 requires rather more core store than GEORGE 1: from three to six thousand 24-bit words. Thus the system is only available for machines with a minimum 32000 words of core store. It also requires so much other equipment and channel or device time that on most medium-sized machines it it not feasible or even possible to do any multigramming other than that afforded by the system. However when properly used and in appropriate circumstances it can achieve better results than multiprogramming, as it works in a more streamlined and organised way. It should therefore be regarded as a disciplined method of using multiprogramming, rather than something to be used in conjunction with, or superimposed on it, on medium-sized machines. On larger machines it would be possible to use a variety of different systems, in a multiprogrammed way, under control of Executive. But to utilise the power of the computer to the best advantage it is more sensible to pool the resources of the systems: not to support several, separate off-line streams, but instead to share them by means of a common file store, as in GEORGE 3.

5

THE GEORGE 3 CONCEPT

TIM GOLDINGHAM

After GEORGE 1 and 2, Tim Goldingham uses GEORGE 3 to illustrate more advanced operating system facilities. He touches lightly on the File Store, and shows how it can be used to provide more flexible off-lining, and Accounting facilities. He then elaborates on the concept of Multiaccess, including its use for program development, and introduces the idea of conversational compilers. Finally he discusses the important question of scheduling.

5.1 Introduction

The GEORGE 3 Operating System for the ICL 1900 Series is a comprehensive system combining both batch processing and multi-access facilities. It is thus considerably more ambitious than the GEORGE 1 and 2 systems referred to in previous chapters: while these were single-stream systems, controlling a single set of programs, GEORGE 3 takes control of the entire machine.

To understand the design concepts, it may be helpful to consider the predicament of the human operator. He is required:

(a) to interpret programmer's instructions
(b) to type the corresponding messages on the console
(c) to set up the basic peripherals—card readers, printers, etc.
(d) to keep these peripherals permanently supplied with the appropriate fodder—cards, paper, etc.
(e) to set up magnetic peripherals—tapes, and discs
(f) to keep a log of everything that happens, so that users can be charged
(g) and, in his spare time, to determine what mixture of jobs will make the best use of both central processor and peripherals.

To maintain this performance throughout a shift requires a superhuman degree of both physical and mental stamina. Yet most of the tasks listed are, in fact, relatively simple routine operations—just the things we are told computers are good at. It is eminently sensible, therefore, to ask the machine to perform as many of them as possible.

5.2 The File Store

We have already seen in chapter 4 how GEORGE 1 and 2 in fact assist with some of these tasks. By providing a Command Language they cater for the interpretation of instructions: by off-lining peripheral input and output they simplify the handling of basic peripherals. What more can be done?

The answer lies in the provision of a FILE STORE. The object of this is to ensure that all the information required by the system is permanently available to it. The File Store is held primarily on some direct access device, though it may overflow on to magnetic tapes, and is organised in a hierarchical structure. Files within it may contain basically one of three types of information. The first is data, organised in whatever manner may be appropriate for the user's requirements; for some jobs a serial organisation will be appropriate, while for others a direct access file may be required. The second is programs, in either source or compiled form. The third is concerned purely with the organization of the File Store itself: certain files will be required to hold Directories which indicate the contents of other files below them in the hierarchy.

The detailed operation of the File Store is, deservedly, the subject of a separate chapter, and will not be expanded here; but it is fundamental to an understanding of the concept of George 3 since many other facilities are derived from it.

5.3 Input-Output

Consider for instance the handling of input and output. There are three ways in which this may be handled in George 3. The most straightforward is simple on-line connexion of the peripheral to the user program. This, however, requires the continuous attention of the operator which we are attempting to avoid, and will therefore only be resorted to when there is some special requirement such as the use of a non-standard data code.

Much commoner will be some form of OFF-LINING. Chapter 4 explained how this is handled by George 2, where the sequence of processing is the same as that of input. Thanks to the File Store, George 3 can adopt a more flexible approach: batches of input can be stored away in files, and accessed as required. Thus the data for a particular job may be fed in during the morning, and not processed until the afternoon.

There is a distinction to be made between two methods of achieving this. In one, a named file is created to hold a batch of input. The command

INPUT peripheral name, file name

can then be issued within a Job Description, and the data will be read into that file. It will then be necessary to connect this file to the appropriate user program. This is done by means of the ASSIGN command. In the job description to run the program, the programmer writes, for example,

ASSIGN * CR0, INPUTDATA

The effect of this will be that whenever a Card Read instruction is encountered within the program, it will be intercepted by GEORGE and converted into an instruction to extract a record from the file named. Similarly, the command

ASSIGN * LP0, OUTPUT

will ensure that all printer output is not listed directly on the line printer, but stored in the file named OUTPUT to be printed later.

The second method of off-lining is similar, but employs temporary instead of permanent files. The OFFLINE command is used to convert a job to this mode of operation: a temporary file is automatically created, and erased as soon as its contents have been used.

5.4 Accounting

Another facility associated with the File Store is that of Accounting. A general-purpose system to be used by a variety of users for many different purposes must provide a means for debiting each such user with the cost of the facilities he has employed. For this purpose George 3 sets up a monitoring file for every job that is run. This file stores in effect the details of the progress of the job which in an operator-controlled environment would have been output on the console typewriter—core store occupied, mill time, peripherals used, etc. At the completion of the job a Log Analysis program is called in to analyse these details and produce for the user a statement of the cost incurred. In addition, the monitoring file may if desired be preserved for further consolidated analysis.

Such an accounting system goes some way towards providing the control which the Installation Manager requires. It is, however, purely historical: to close the stable door while the horse is still safely inside, a Budgeting system is required. This again is only possible because of the existence of the hierarchical File Store in which are recorded details of all users of the system.

Whenever a User creates subordinates within the file store, he must allocate to them a share of his budget. Budgets are for three resources: Space, Time, and Money.

The treatment of these is slightly different. Space and Time budgets are enforced when other users require access to the system: thus a user will be permitted access to a certain area of file store as his Space Budget. If he wishes to use more space he will be permitted to do so as long as it is vacant; but as soon as another user requires it he will be confined to the area permitted by his budget. Similar considerations apply to the Time budget: he will be allowed to use the central processor for as long as he likes (subject to his Money budget), provided that by doing so he is not interfering with other users.

The over-riding constraint is the Money budget, which can never be exceeded. This of course is related to the financial units used in the Log Analysis program, which are set by the Installation Manager. Thus, use of mill time will be charged at so much a minute: there will be a rate for use of each type of peripheral, together with a setting-up charge; and occupancy of both core and file store will be charged at a rate per thousand words per minute. By adjusting these rates the Installation Manager can influence users, for instance, to use one type of input peripheral rather than another, according to the facilities most in demand. Further elaborations are possible, for instance the setting of differential rates for prime shift working.

The user's budget is checked at the start of each job, whether it is submitted through a multiaccess console or as a background job: if the budget has been exceeded, the job cannot proceed until further resources are granted by the user's superior.

Resources are allocated on a periodic (normally monthly) basis: thus a user will be permitted a certain expenditure each month, and if he has exhausted his allowance for the current month he must wait till the start of the next one for his job to be run. The extent to which he is allowed to carry over his budget from one month to the next is under the control of the Installation Manager. Each user is assigned a Ration: this is the amount of money allocated to him *per month*. The actual figure he can spend in the current month is called his *allowance*, which will consist of his ration augmented by whatever proportion of the unexpired balance of the previous months ration he may have been allowed to carry forward—this might be set at one-half for instance. Thus if his monthly ration were £100 and in the first month of using the system he spent only £80, his *allowance* for the second month would be £110 [£100 + $\frac{1}{2}$ (£100–£80)].

This budgeting facility is of particular importance in a *multiaccess* environment, in which a large number of users have access to the computer from remote terminals, and so cannot be subjected to the controls that can be applied to work sent into the machine room.

5.5 Multiaccess

Chapter 4 suggested the maximisation of the number of simultaneous users as one of the possible aims of an operating system. Some operating systems are designed specifically for this purpose, while others confine themselves to batch processing. In the case of GEORGE 3 it was one of the fundamental design aims that the system should provide equally for both types of usage, employing as far as possible the same command language for both types of work. We should therefore be clear on what is meant by multiaccess.

The fundamental problem in the effective use of computers is the fantastic imbalance between the speed of the electronic central processor and the mechanical peripherals. It is this that gives rise to the concept of multiprogramming, as the processor is quite capable of driving several sets of peripherals simultaneously. Even so, however, it is rarely fully occupied: further capacity is still available if we can find the means of using it.

This is not practicable in terms of normal batch processing: most jobs of this kind require several peripherals, and it would be uneconomic to provide the quantity that would be needed. But in any case, is batch processing the best means of using a computer?

The reason why we process data in batches is again to be found in the imbalance of speed already referred to: it was thought that the way to keep the central processor occupied was to feed data to it at the fastest possible rate, by loading large quantities of data into very fast peripherals. This is ideal for many commercial applications; but it is by no means always what we want to do with our computers. If we really want to use them for computing we may have only a limited amount of data to work on: furthermore, we may not be too sure at the start of the job what we want to do with this data. In other words, we want to develop our program as we go along, inspecting intermediate results and deciding on subsequent steps when these have been analysed.

The sort of implement we require then, is not a fast card or paper tape reader but a typewriter—something more closely geared to normal human speeds of operation. But how can we afford to harness our hare-like processor to such a tortoise? We can still do this economically provided we attach a large number of typewriters. Now we can really keep the central processor busy, and at the same time satisfy a gratifyingly large number of users, each of whom can sit contentedly at his console under the impression that he has control of the entire computer—just as the cinemagoer is oblivious of the fact that for much of the time he is staring at a blank screen. This is the concept of multiaccess.

We have been representing multiaccess and batch processing as diametrically opposed: but it is quite possible to combine them in one system, and this is in fact what GEORGE 3 sets out to do. The system is designed so that as far as possible the two types of work are handled in the same way, using the same Command Language.

Let us imagine a user seated one day at his console—not, we hope, too ill at ease—and see how he operates.

The first thing he must do is to 'log-in'—to establish his connexion with the computer, and his authority to use it. He therefore types

LOGIN followed by the current Job Name and his User Name, and awaits the machine's response.

This will depend on the number of other users: a limit is set on the total number of jobs that can be run, and he may receive message that this has already been reached. If this is not the case GEORGE will proceed to examine his User Name.

A full understanding of the significance of this name must await the explanation of the File Store in chapter 7: suffice it to say for the moment that each user's name is registered when he is first admitted to the system. Thus when he attempts to log in from his console, a check can be made against the File Store's dictionary to ensure that he is a recognised user.

This check is not, however, sufficient to prevent any unauthorised interloper from posing as a named user: the next step is therefore for the machine to print TYPE PASSWORD on the typewriter, to which the user must reply with a unique password, known only to himself and GEORGE.

The precise methods of controlling this check vary between multiaccess systems; installations which are particularly concerned to prevent unauthorised access may have typewriters on which printing can be suppressed, so that the password cannot be read; or the typewriter may backspace after each character so that nothing appears but a black square. Alternatively, physical controls such as a lock on the keyboard can be fitted. These have the disadvantage that a user may not be able to transfer to another keyboard if his own is unserviceable. All these devices will, of course, increase the costs of the hardware, and are not provided on the standard 1900 installation.

Our user, then, has established his credentials: can he now be given unrestricted access to the machine? There is unfortunately still one further most important constraint—that of budget. As explained earlier, a budget limit is set by the Installation Manager on the resources which each user may employ, and this is checked each time he logs in.

Assuming that he has satisfied all these checks, the user is now able to do from his console virtually anything that he could do by submitting a job to be run in the machine room. He can for instance type job descriptions on his console, using the standard command language. He can create new programs by typing each instruction line by line and have them run or stored in the file store. Equally he can call up an existing program held in the file store by giving the name of that file. Source programs may be altered by the use of a Context Editor, which will locate any desired instruction and make any necessary corrections to it.

When it comes to running his program, the integrated design of GEORGE 3, combining batch processing with multiaccess, enables him to employ various sophisticated techniques for program development. He can, for instance, give instructions for his console to simulate certain input and output peripherals. If, for instance, he gives the command ONLINE*CR0, this will instruct GEORGE 3 that for the purpose of the current program the console is to be substituted for the card reader. Thus every time his program issues a Card Read instruction, instead of the card reader being activated a message will be typed on the console, to which the user must respond by typing 80 characters as they would appear on a card. Alternatively, he may issue an INPUT command from the console, which will write all subsequent messages into a file until the terminator (normally in GEORGE 3 ****) is detected. This file can subsequently be connected to a program by means of the ASSIGN command, again given from the console after the program has been loaded. Output can similarly be diverted to the console by the command ONLINE*LP0 (or*CP0). A necessary feature is the ability to interrupt such output, otherwise it would be possible for an erroneous program to get into a loop and swamp the console in a spate of meaningless verbiage, which could only be checked by abandoning the program altogether. The console user is therefore provided with a Break-in key which allows him to re-establish contact with the Operating System rather than the program. This facility may be used to check a program, make some alteration to it and then continue; alternatively, the user may now decide that he has achieved all that is needed in the inter-active mode, and that he wishes the program to continue to run as a background job while he proceeds with another job. In such a case he can set the program up and then give a DISCONNECT command, which may optionally be followed by the name of a further job; the first job is now removed from the control of the console, and the new one substituted for it.

When the MOP (Multiple On-line Processing) session is finished, the user must sign off by logging out. He may, however, have a program in core which he does not wish to lose: if so, he can give a SAVE command which will cause it to be stored as a saved file: he will then be able to restore and re-enter it by means of a RESUME command. When he finally types LOGOUT his job is removed from the list of active jobs in the system, and the monitoring file is inspected: such details as he requires of the usage he has made of the system, the charges he has incurred and the budget remaining to him are printed on the console.

Further developments of GEORGE 3 enhance its multiaccess facilities. Visual displays can be substituted for typewriters as MOP consoles, and the amount of information available to the console user is increased: for instance, messages intended for one user may be filed by other users and output as soon as he logs in. But the most important development lies in the area of special software for multi-access—in particular, conversational compilers.

5.6 Conversational compilers

A console user can use a conventional compiler to translate a program from source to object form, and subsequently run it. Clearly however he cannot do any testing until his entire program is complete: furthermore, the amount of diagnostic information that he can obtain is limited to a syntax check on each line as it is input. For interactive work it is more satisfactory to interpret each source instruction as it is input and obey it immediately. The user can then scrutinise the result before generating the next instruction. This is made possible by several 'conversational' compilers, often modelled on the JOSS language developed by The Rand Corporation. ICL's version for the 1900 series is known as JEAN, and is described in Chapter 8.

Future compilers are likely to be provided in several different versions. One version will provide fast compiling at the expense of object code efficiency: this will enable the terminal user to develop a program quickly, and when it is proven recompile it using a different compiler, this time designed to give the most efficient object code regardless of compiling speed. This might be done by providing an intermediate language between source and object code, which could be run interpretively. An extension of this concept is to use a satellite computer for multiaccess compilation, using such an interpretive intermediate code, and then to transmit this over a transmission link to a powerful central computer for the second stage of compilation into optimised object code.

Undoubtedly multiaccess offers the most exciting possibilities for extending man-machine communication, and the time will come when every home has its terminal as today it has its telephone.

5.7 Scheduling

There remains the question of Scheduling. We have seen that the Operating System may have a large number of jobs submitted to it by users; and that if it sets out to offer multiaccess facilities it must be able to deal with such jobs at very short notice, to give terminal users a satisfactory response. It must therefore have a means of deciding which jobs to run at any given moment. This is provided by the Scheduler.

Scheduling can be considered at two levels: strategy and tactics. By the latter is meant the millisecond-by-millisecond control of the machine. An understanding of this requires a detailed consideration of the internal workings of the system, which are examined in the next chapter. By strategy is meant the overall selection of jobs, such as might be carried out by a human operator in planning his work for a shift. In fact in the GEORGE 3 system these two are handled by distinct modules, the High Level and Low Level Schedulers.

The factors considered by the High Level Scheduler can in turn be divided into two categories: those that relate to the configuration of machine being used, and those related to the program being run. The former include such factors as:

(a) the core store available for programs
(b) the proportion of multiaccess to background work
(c) the maximum number of jobs to be allowed in the system
(d) the backing store transfer rate
(e) the peripherals available.

Some of these must be determined by the installation manager, who has to strike a balance between providing a rapid service to terminal users and ensuring that background jobs are not unduly delayed.

As far as individual programs are concerned factors to be considered include

(a) the urgency of the job—indicated in GEORGE 3 by a letter A–Z
(b) the time by which it must be finished (the 'Deadline')
(c) the estimated run time
(d) the availability of the necessary files and on-line peripherals
(e) the size of the program
(f) whether the program is likely to be limited by core store or by peripherals.

Some programs, dealing with real time situations, will need to be retained permanently in core, and never swapped out.

Commands are provided in GEORGE 3 by which all these items can be communicated to the Operating System, either as pre-set parameters or within the job description. The precise algorithm used to evaluate them and make a choice of programs will often vary from one installation to another: a machine providing primarily an open-shop computing service for an engineering laboratory will have different needs from a predominantly batch-processing commercial installation. Facilities are therefore provided within GEORGE 3 for users to write their own High Level Scheduler and incorporate it into the System in place of the standard module.

Whether the High Level Scheduler is written by the user or supplied by the manufacturer, the end product in the case of GEORGE 3 is a Computing Power Index for each program. This is a figure which indicates the proportion of the next time-slice which that program should be allowed to occupy. This calculation is made approximately every minute, and the resulting list of programs to be run, with their CPIs, is passed to the Low Level Scheduler. This is entered more frequently (about once per second) and assigns to each program a Time Slot dependent on the size of the program and the total number of programs active. It also computes an Ideal Waiting Time, based on the CPI, the time slot, the length of the last run, and the number of background jobs that are waiting. The next program to be run at any given moment is then the one which has the greatest discrepancy between its Ideal Waiting Time and the time it has actually been waiting.

Finally, programs are run by being 'plugged in' to Executive, so that the lowest level of control is exercised in the normal multi-programming manner. In the next chapter we will examine how programs are run in more detail.

6

GEORGE 3 INTERNAL WORKING

TIM GOLDINGHAM

Having introduced the more advanced concepts of George 3, Tim Goldingham now examines its workings in greater detail. He describes the organisation of core store, and the manner in which Chaining is used to provide a completely flexible system. He then considers further one of the most important chains, that containing information about Activities, and this leads to an understanding of the way in which the total control of the various processes in the operating system takes place. Finally, he illustrates this by examining an actual situation in detail.

6.1 Fundamental principles

The previous chapter was concerned with GEORGE 3 as it appears to the user. We now examine the internal functioning of the System.

Certain fundamental principles can be isolated. Firstly, the positioning of the interface. We have already seen that GEORGE is an independent piece of software in the sense that compilers and applications packages are freestanding; they are not built into the 1900 Operating System as is done with some other systems, but are written to the same interface as user programs.

In the other direction, an interface is defined between the Operating System and Executive. In this way the modules required to handle all possible peripherals configurations can be included in Executive, so that a single version of GEORGE 3 itself can be run on many different 1900s.

The second decision that was made in the early stages of the design was that GEORGE 3 should not be interruptable: that is to say that when an external event occurs, GEORGE does not service it immediately, but is notified of it and deals with it at the next convenient moment. We shall see that these two features require an efficient means of communication between Executive and GEORGE and a mechanism for allocating time slots of a comparatively short duration, so that peripheral incidents are handled without delay.

A third design aim was a completely flexible system of core store management, to avoid the inefficiencies which inevitably result if any particular portion of core is earmarked for a particular purpose.

Finally, it was agreed that GEORGE should be coded as a number of pure procedures—i.e. that routines should not be changed during execution so that it is possible for the same routines to be used by more than one process.

6.2 Core store organization

Figure 1 illustrates the core store of a 1900 processor using GEORGE 3.

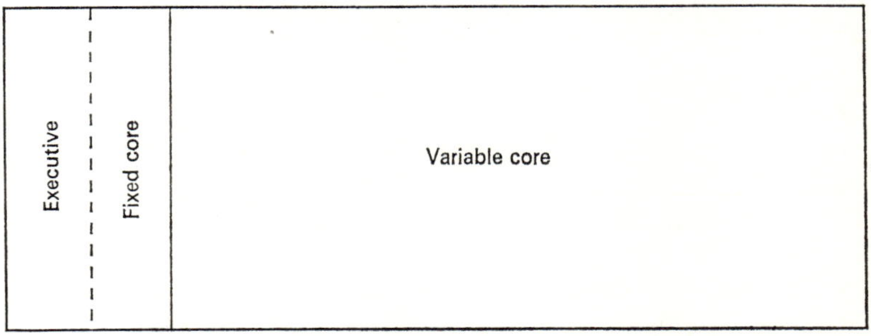

Fig. 1

As usual on 1900s the lowest-numbered locations are occupied by Executive; but in this instance the line indicating the boundary of executive is shown dotted, since (as mentioned above) there is communication between Executive and the Operating System, so that the dividing line between them is less sharp than between Executive and a user program. The GEORGE 3 Executive is specially written for use with the Operating System and cannot be used in any other environment: conversely, GEORGE 3 cannot run with any other executive.

The area marked as Fixed Core contains portions of GEORGE 3 which must be permanently in core. The combined Executive and Fixed Core can therefore be regarded as corresponding to a Standard Executive, and in fact their core requirement (about 12 000 words) would be no greater than that of a standard Executive for a large configuration.

The remainder of core, shown in Figure 1 as Variable, is occupied by user programs and GEORGE as required. GEORGE 3 itself consists of some 100 000 words of code: this is divided into *Chapters* of variable length (normally less than 1000 words); at any given moment Variable Core will contain a number of such chapters, containing the code required for the current operations, and also a number of user programs with their data. GEORGE can thus be compared with an overlaid super-executive. The mechanism for swapping chapters into core is known as the Chapter Changer, and is present in Fixed Core.

6.3 Chaining

The basic multiprogramming system of the 1900 Series provides for relocation of programs, so that whenever a program is deleted the remaining programs are moved down in core making all free space contiguous. This is illustrated in Figure 2, where the second diagram shows the core allocation after program B has been deleted.

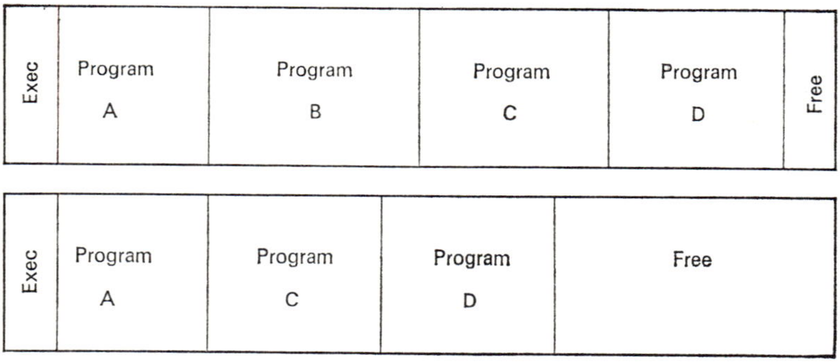

Fig. 2.

Such a system is ideal for a batch processing machine of limited core size, but would be unacceptable for a large core in a multiaccess environment where programs are being swapped frequently and much movement would be necessary; furthermore, it would not be practicable to move chapters of GEORGE about in this way. The core management system adopted is therefore one of *chaining*, as illustrated in Figure 3.

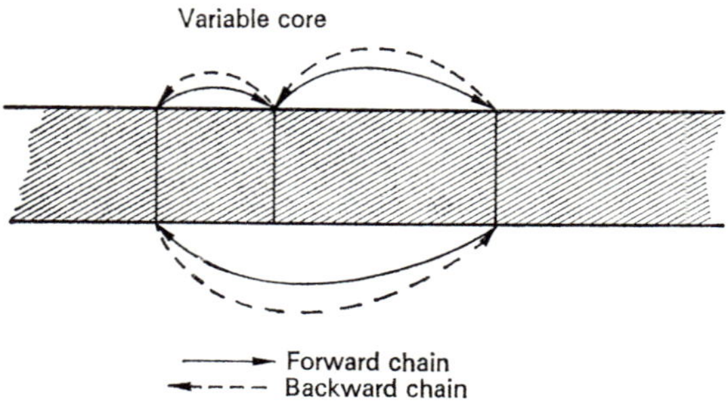

Fig. 3.

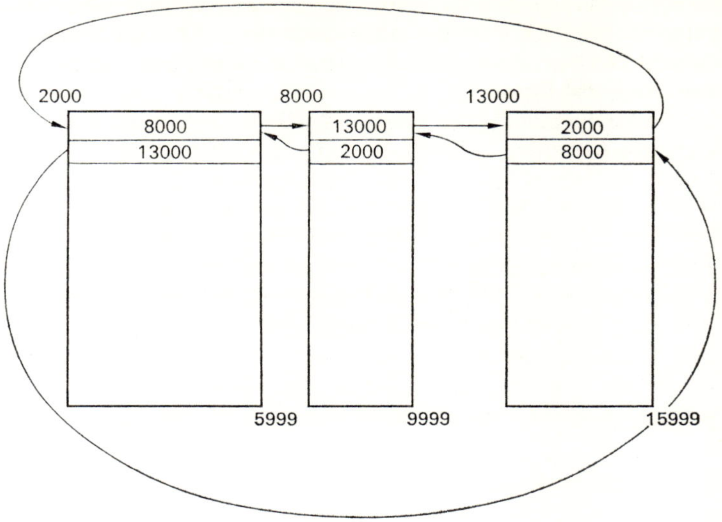

Fig. 4.

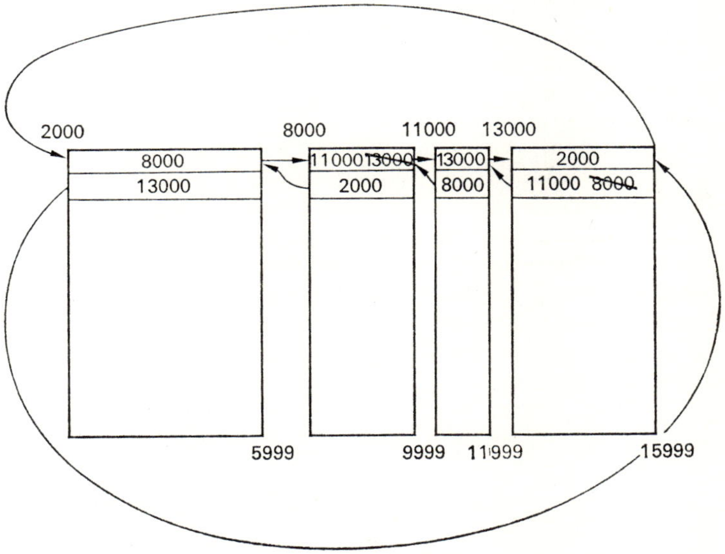

Fig. 5.

Blocks may be anywhere in core*; each block has in its first two locations pointers *forward* to the next block in the chain, and *backward* to the previous block (the last block pointing to the first and

*The diagram is not strictly accurate, since any core is one dimensional, and one block would of course occupy consecutively numbered locations.

vice versa, to complete the chain). There are a large number of such chains in GEORGE 3; together (including the Free Store Chain which links all unoccupied blocks) they account for the whole of core store. Figure 4 illustrates the principle expressed this time in terms of addresses; while Figure 5 demonstrates the ease with which a new block can be added to a chain: this operation involves no movement in core, simply the alteration of a couple of pointers.

One of the portions of GEORGE 3 which is contained in Fixed Core is the Core Allocation System, which searches the Free Core Chain whenever core is required either for a chapter of GEORGE or for a user program. Also within Fixed Core are the Chain Base Pairs containing the forward and backward pointers which provide access to the various chains.

With an understanding of this Chaining Technique, we can examine one of the most important chains in the system.

6.4 The activity chain

GEORGE 3 is required to perform many functions—loading programs, handling peripheral transfers, etc. Every such function can be called an Activity. At any time, it is likely that GEORGE will be carrying out a number of such activities; and since they are often held up, for instance while awaiting the completion of a transfer, they can be multiprogrammed in the normal manner. This is illustrated in Figure 6.

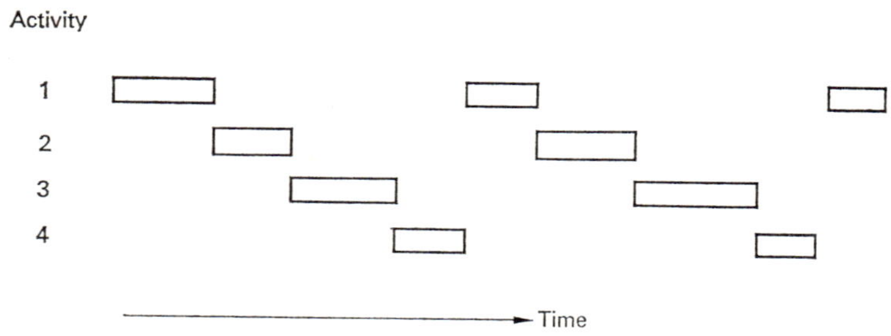

Fig. 6.

The actual code to perform any such activity is contained in Chapters of GEORGE: any one activity may require several chapters. But, as stated earlier, these chapters are *pure*: that is, one chapter may be used by several activities.

We thus have the situation illustrated in Figure 7, which develops Figure 6 to show how the same *Chapter* may be employed by several *activities*, while each *activity* employs several *chapters*.

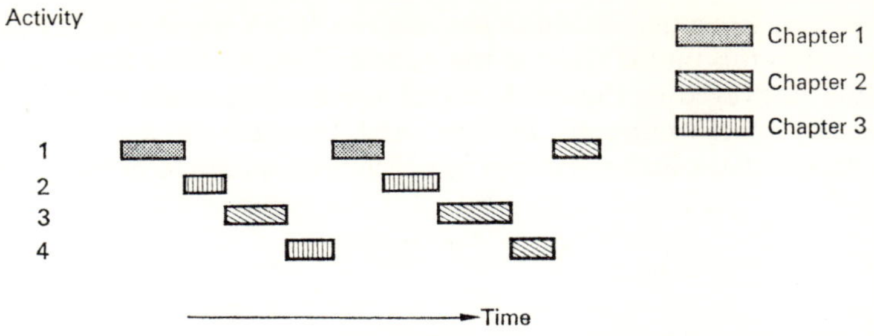

Fig. 7.

Though the chapters themselves are pure, there must of course be variable information associated with each Activity. This is held in an *activity block*: activity blocks are linked together in a chain known as the *activity chain*. Thus the activity is an abstract name describing the process; the variable information associated with it is contained in an activity block in the activity chain, and its code in one or more chapters. The activity block may also have some data blocks associated with it.

The layout of the Activity Block is shown in Figure 8, from which it will be seen that it contains a cross-reference to the related chapter: conversely, the first word in each chapter records the activity which it is currently processing.

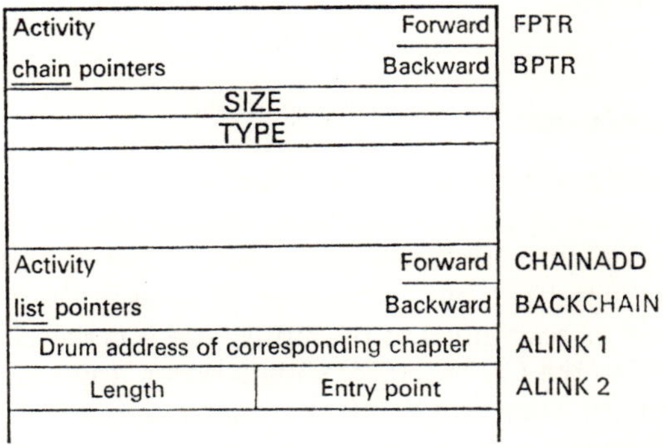

Fig. 8.

We have seen how the Activity Chain links all the activity blocks in core at any time. We now have to consider the scheduling mechanism which provides communication with Executive. In addition to the activity chain, there is also an *activity list*. This is in fact a two-way chain, like the activity chain, but differs from it in that it contains only those activity blocks which require servicing. Whenever an interrupt occurs to Executive, for instance because of a peripheral incident, Executive identifies the Activity Block which can handle it and adds this on the front of the Activity List. We have thus the situation portrayed in Figure 9, where the activity *chain* contains all activity blocks currently in core, and the activity *list* threads a subset of these, in the sequence in which they require to be processed.

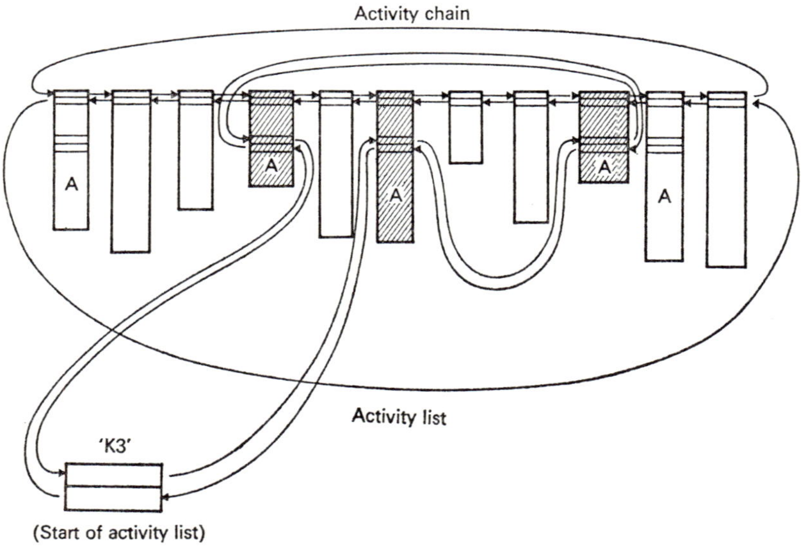

Fig. 9.

6.5 The Co-ordinator

The mechanism which picks these activities off the list for processing, is known as the Co-ordinator, and a simplified flow chart of it is shown in Figure 10. It was stated earlier that 'GEORGE should not be interruptable': but, of course, it is essential that external events should be responded to promptly, and it is therefore arranged that an entry to the Co-ordinator should occur approximately every 100 instructions. Thus GEORGE is not interrupted, but breaks off at frequent intervals to review the situation to see what most urgently needs attention. Study of the flow chart will show how it takes the top item from the activity list, and puts the current item back on the bottom. In this way the situation portrayed in Figure 6 is achieved.

Looking first at entry 1 ('Regular'), we see the procedure followed when an activity is interrupted when it has not yet been completed, but has reached the end of its 'time slot'. The next instruction to be obeyed is dumped in the word known as ALINK 2, which (Figure 8) indicates the entry point, and the block is put on the end of the Activity List, so that in due course its turn will come round again.

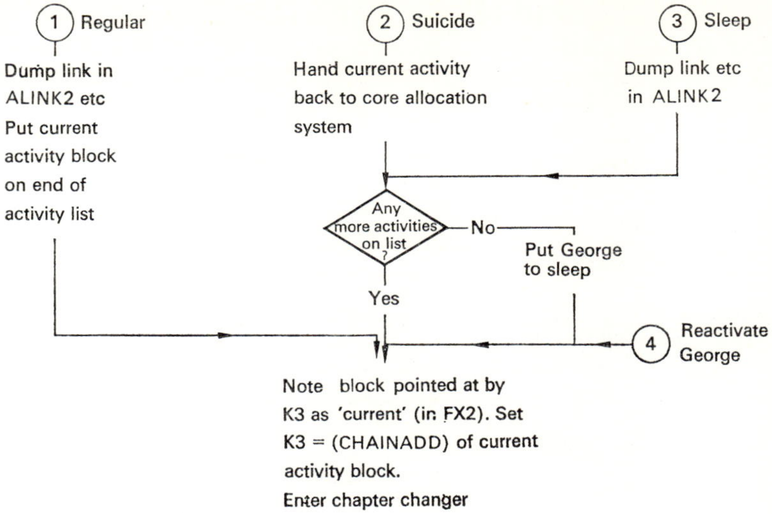

Fig. 10.

The block pointed at by the 'Start of Activity List' location now becomes the 'Current' activity, and the Start of List location is set to the contents of its 'Chainadd' word—i.e. to what was the *second* block in the list. In this way the next block on the list is entered whenever an activity's time slot is completed.

It may be, however, that the activity has in fact terminated. In this case we enter the flowchart at entry 2 ('Suicide'), and hand the space it occupied back to the Core Allocation System, so that it can be used for further activities. We then examine the List to see if there are any more activities awaiting processing, and if so enter them as before: if there are none, GEORGE can be made inactive.

The third entry ('Sleep') applies to those cases where the activity still has more work to do, and has not completed its time slot, but cannot continue processing because it is waiting for the completion of some other action, most often the transfer of information to or from a peripheral. In this case it drops to the back of the queue, and an entry will be caused to the Co-ordinator when the transfer is completed.

6.6 Typical situation

Having explained the principles on which GEORGE operates, let us examine an actual situation—for instance the processing of a simple Job Description to load and enter a program. This is illustrated in Figure 11.

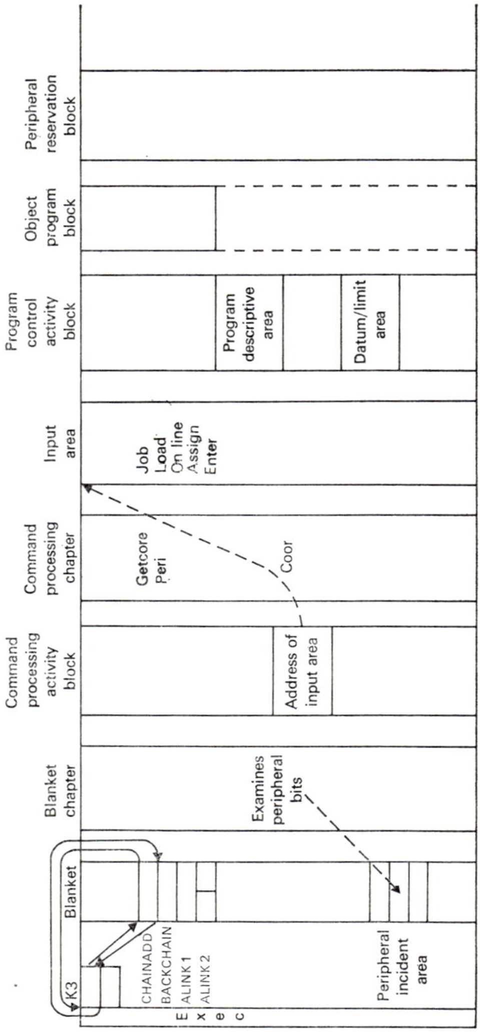

Fig. 11.

The operator loads the card reader with the job description cards, followed by the program and the data, and presses the ENGAGE button. This will cause an interrupt, which is detected by the Blanket activity which is permanently resident in core. Within this Blanket activity is a three-word area known as the Peripheral Incident Area, in which one bit is allocated to each peripheral attached to the processor: thus when the card reader is engaged, a bit will be set corresponding to this particular device. Blanket will recognise that the interrupt which called it in was produced by a peripheral, and will call in the Chapter of GEORGE responsible for the processing of peripheral incidents. This will examine the Peripheral Incident Area to determine which peripheral caused the interrupt: having established that this was the card reader, it will call in a further activity, known as the Command Processing Activity.

The Command Processing Activity calls in the Command Processing Chapter from backing store, to achieve the reading in of a card image. For this purpose a buffer area will be required: the Command Processing Chapter obtains this through the core allocation system, and places its address within the Command Processing Activity. It can then issue a peripheral transfer instruction referring to this address.

While this transfer instruction is taking place, the Activity will be suspended. This is the reason for having separate Activities to handle the various peripherals: this may at first sight appear an unnecessarily complex process, but it is necessary if time-sharing of peripherals is to be achieved. Cards are read in from the card reader into an 80-character buffer area, and thence transferred to a Job Description File which is created in the file-store. This file is then analysed by the Command Processing Activity.

It is likely that the first instruction will be to LOAD a program. To achieve this, further blocks will be required: a Program Control Activity, an Object Program block to hold the program and a Peripheral Reservation Block.

The Program Control Activity Block contains details of the program, notably its datum and limit which describe to Executive the area in core store which it will occupy. It is, in fact, the means by which Executive obtains the information it needs to run the program.

The Object Program Block is initially only large enough to hold the first 100 or so words of program, which are loaded in when the LOAD command is processed. This command is likely to be followed by commands describing the peripherals required for running the program. These may be connected directly to the program, in which case the ONLINE command is used; alternatively they may be simulated through the file store, so that when the program gives for instance a card read instruction, it is intercepted by GEORGE and translated into instructions to read a card record from a file which has already been set up in the File Store. In this case, the ASSIGN command is used.

Details of these peripheral allocations are recorded in two-word entries in the Peripheral Reservation Block; in the case of off-line peripherals, these contain pointers to a further Off-Line Peripheral Activity Block.

We are now ready to run the program. To do this, a reference to the program must be made in the job list of a routine known as the Low Level Scheduler.

The Low Level Scheduler is entered at regular intervals. Knowing the total core available, it examines the properties of all the programs in its program list and decides which jobs should actually be run. Details of these, in the form of the addresses of their Program Control Blocks, are passed across to Executive for running in the same way as with a normal multiprogramming Executive.

This chapter has given an outline of the manner in which GEORGE 3 communicates with Executive, and handles a number of time-shared activities, essentially on a 'round-robin' system. One point requires a little further amplification—the means of communication with the Filestore, which was touched on in connexion with the reading in of the Job Description.

It was stated that cards are read into an 80-character buffer. There would also be a larger buffer, 512 words long, into which these records would be transferred. When this buffer in turn becomes full, it must be transferred to backing store.

Associated with each Activity is a File Control Block which records details of its files. These include the name of each file, together with a list showing the backing store address of each of the 512-word blocks which go to make up that file. Thus when the buffer becomes full it may be stored in any convenient place on backing store.

However, we are anticipating the explanation of the Filestore which is the subject of the next chapter.

7

THE GEORGE 3 FILE STORE

ANGUS BEATTY

As was pointed out in Chapter 5, one of the most important aspects of GEORGE 3 is its File store, and Angus Beatty discusses this in greater depth. He refers to the various types of file which occupy it, and explains the hierarchal manner in which it is structured, including its relevance to Accounting. Next he discusses the concept of Privacy, very important in a multiaccess environment, and finally describes the facilities for dumping, both for handling file overflow and for allowing retrieval in the event of system breakdown.

7.1 General

As we saw in Chapter 6, there are two modes of running programs under the control of the GEORGE 3 operating system; under direct control from a remote console, or as a background job. This division categorises the means by which the program *instructions* are initiated and their execution monitored. There is equally a distinction to be made between the two ways in which a program of either type may access its data: the two varieties of file allowed are *on-line files* and *files in the file store*. The most obvious external difference between the two is that an on-line file seems to its user (and actually is) resident on a specific external peripheral such as paper tape or disc at the moment of time in the execution of the object program when an access occurs. A user's data file in the file store, on the other hand, although also appearing to an object program to reside on backing store, is in general partly in core and partly on direct access backing store at the moment when the operating system executes an object program access instruction. Subject to certain restrictions which are stated later in this chapter, the user accesses such a file just as he would an on-line file.

The implementation details are that executive reports to the operating system proper whenever a user program opens or accesses a file of either type. The operating system itself then deals with references to a file in the file store: for example, if an object program writes a 'block of paper tape' to a file in the file store then the operating system will transfer the output data from the user program's buffer to another (system) buffer in core. Thence at convenient intervals the operating system will transfer blocks of data from the system buffer to the direct access backing store used for file storage.

The advantages of using files of this type wherever practicable are clear. The system gains because it does not suffer the traditional bottleneck of multiprogramming systems: the lack of enough peripherals attached to the installation. Even in a large installation with, say, two card readers and two line printers it was not previously possible for more than two programs to be multiprogrammed together if each needed a card reader and line printer. Thus such a system without a file store suffered either from lack of full utilisation of the central processor or from the necessity for the user to contort natural methods of program testing and production running in order to minimise usage of peripherals. But by exploiting the file store the user programmer may use the 'peripheral' best suited to his application and leave all the problems of timesharing, scheduling, and data file storage to the operating system.

For simplicity, the word *file* as used in the rest of this chapter has the meaning 'a file in the GEORGE 3 file store.'

It should be noted that the filestore contains, besides the type of file so far described, files containing *programs* accessed by the operating system or by system software such as loader programs. This is a matter of convenience for the operating system and system software, and because of the arrangements for naming (see below) an applications programmer does not have to bother about the fact that his program's data is sharing the use of the operating system's file store with these other files (such as the library file) of which he has no knowledge. Another example of a set of system files which occupy the file store is a temporary file which the user causes the operating system to form when he writes an OFFLINE command in his job description (see chapter 5). In the case of an input file the operating system then reads all the file concerned into a temporary file in the file store ready to be offered on demand, a record at a time, to the object program. The area of file store occupied by such a file can be re-allocated for other purposes by the operating system when the program has closed the file or been deleted.

The operating system is also able to move a file about the file store, if necessary because of the changing core store and backing store requirements of other user programs or of the operating system itself.

7.2 File Types

7.2.1 Serial File

This is a file analagous to an off-line paper tape or card file. The user may read 'the next' record from a serial input file or write 'the next' record to a serial output file. The format of a serial file is actually card-like or paper tape-like and a consistent set of read and write instructions must be used by the object program to access it.

A serial file may also be handled as 'magnetic tape', provided that only open, read, write, or close operations are performed on it.

7.2.2 Direct Access File

This type of file is analagous to a disc file. That is to say the user has complete flexibility of the order in which he accesses it: typically, a number of words may be read from or written to any word address in the file in consecutive 'peripheral' transfers.

7.2.3 Communication File

Any direct access file may be opened by more than one program simultaneously for reading only. However, a *communication file* is a serial file which is open for reading by one program and at the same time by another for writing. The typical case is for a program to be adding data to the end of a file while another program is reading through the file some way behind. If the reading program attempts to read off the end of the useful data in the file, the operating system queues its transfer requests until the writing program has written more data. In practice when this condition occurs the data is passed across, as it becomes available, direct in core. If a user writes data to a non-communication serial file, the operating system batches up the records and writes them to backing store: when the user reads such a file later he causes the operating system to do a series of backing store read instructions. This is also the effect in a user programming system which employs a communication file for which the reading program lags behind the writing process. However, in the case where the reading program snaps up data as soon as it is generated by the writing program, no backing store read instruction need be effected by the operating system. Using this method, therefore, peripheral transfer time may be saved.

Communication files enable a user to code his programming system as self-contained, independently compiled *programs*, rather than subroutines consolidated together.

7.3 File Store Structure

The file store as it appears to GEORGE 3 is a single logical entity containing as mentioned above, both system files and user files. These are arranged in a hierarchical (tree) structure. The nodes of the tree are either *directory* (administrative) nodes or actual data (*terminal files*). The user does not have to be aware of the super-structure above the level of his current files unless his application demands it: when writing a program which does not need to exploit

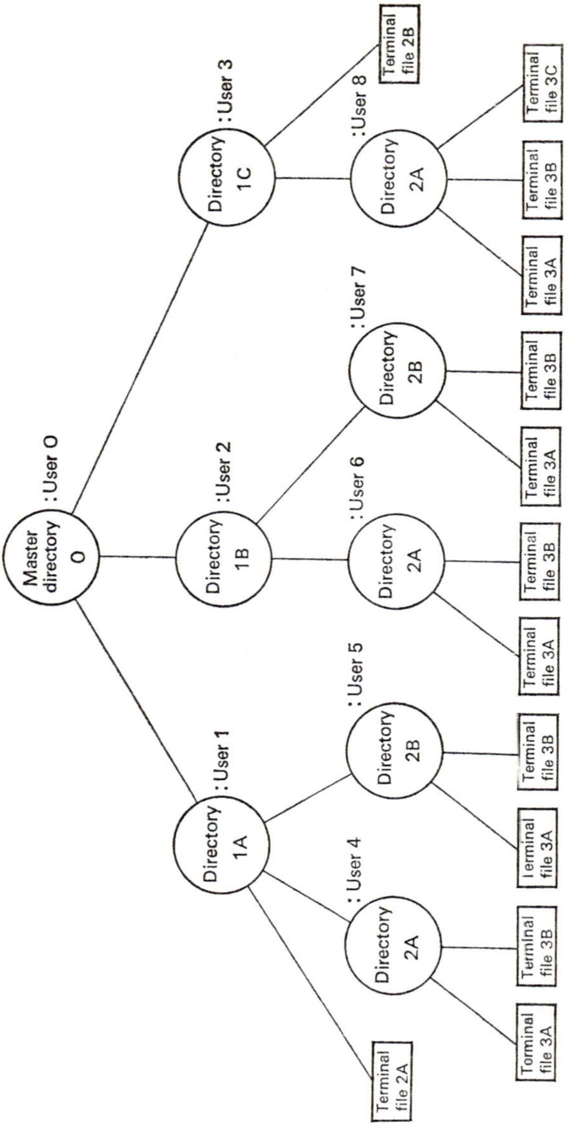
Master directory 0
:User 0
Directory 1A
:User 1
Directory 1B
:User 2
Directory 1C
:User 3
Terminal file 2A
Directory 2A
: User 4
Directory 2B
: User 5
Directory 2A
:User 6
Directory 2B
:User 7
Directory 2A
:User 8
Terminal file 2B
Torminal file 3A
Terminal file 3B
Terminal file 3A
Terminal file 3B
Terminal file 3A
Terminal file 3B
Terminal file 3A
Terminal file 3B
Terminal file 3A
Terminal file 3B
Terminal file 3C

Fig. 12.

the hierarchical structure he can use a subset of the facilities described below. An example of the file store structure is given in Fig. 12.

The DIRECTORY command is available in the GEORGE 3 job description to allow the user to specify which directory he is using as a base-point for identifying the files used in this program. As a default option the user's current directory is assumed to be his *proper directory* which is one of a set of system administrative directories, one per system user. The name of each user's proper directory and other information about him, such as his budget, is stored in a system file known as the *user dictionary.*

A file may be referred to in one of two ways:

1. *Local Name*

   If a single file name is specified in the user's job description, it refers to the terminal file of that name which resides in the file store hierarchy, immediately below the user's current directory.

2. *Absolute Name*

   This is a file name qualified by a user name. By using an absolute name a user may refer to a file immediately below the proper directory of another system user, who has informed the operating system that this is in order.

7.3.1 Links

The LINK command allows the user to refer, by a name private to the current program, to any file in the file store to which he is entitled to have access. For example:

LINK SALARY : PERSONNEL.WAGES

This command would cause the operating system to access the file WAGES belonging to the user PERSONNEL whenever the file name SALARY is referred to in any user's current program. The LINK command causes the operating system to set up an entry in the user's proper directory for the name SALARY pointing to the file WAGES. Note that no duplication of the actual WAGES data is implied.

The LINK option allows a user to write a program operating on files whose file name, owner, and depth in the owner's hierarchy of files, are liable to change during the life of the program.

7.3.2 Streams

STREAM ACCOUNTS, DEBITS + CREDITS + BALANCE

would be an instruction to the operating system to take a reference to the data file ACCOUNTS to be a reference to the three files DEBIT, CREDIT and BALANCE taken in logical serial sequence. This feature might also be used, for example, to offer to a compiler several segments of source program, written as convenient logical units. The files logically joined together by the STREAM facility are presented to the user as a continuous stream of records so that he is not aware of the 'welding' between them.

7.4 Accounting and the File Store

Since the proper directories, one per user, are physically ordinary nodes in the file store it is possible to establish a hierarchy not only of data but of users. Each user has assigned by the installation manager an allocation of money and space, and of CPU time under various priority headings. The relevance of the file store's hierarchical nature to this system is that a user may subdivide his allocations of these three resources to users who come below him in the file store hierarchy. When they use resources, these are automatically charged to the 'superior' user's account.

7.5 Privacy

When a file is initially set up, the user who created it is allowed to access it in any way he pleases. At any time no other user may access it. However, once, the file is set up, the user may authorise other users to access 'his' file in one or more ways, e.g. to read it only, to add to it only, to obey it as a program only, or (say) to access it in all these ways and also to write to it. The operating system will not allow any access to the file except to a user, or hierarchical group of users authorized by the file's 'owner' and then only by the access methods specified by the 'owner'. The owner may use this same system as a means of disciplining his own programs, chiefly as a protection against error.

The GEORGE 3 system also allows protection in the particularly awkward case of the user of an off-line *program*. The problem here is that forgery of any 'credentials' punched on cards or paper tape is very easy. The option is therefore available for a user to despatch his off line program to the machine as a normal remote job, but to declare to the operating system that he wishes to *initiate* a certain program only after logging in *on-line*, at which time he will present his confidential password.

7.6 Dumping

Dumping is effected by GEORGE 3 for two different reasons. These are *file store overflow* and *system breakdown protection*. The dumping and restoring is done by three system programs known as the *incremental dumper*, the *file store* routine, and the *dumper processor*.

7.6.1 Incremental Dumper

The incremental dumper makes a copy of *two* magnetic tapes (in case one develops a fault) of all on-line files in the filestore which have not been already dumped in their current form. An *increment number* associated with each invocation of the dumper is placed in the directory entry of a file as it is dumped, to facilitate the restoring process if this is necessary. The GEORGE 3 system keeps a record of the whereabouts of the two copies of each increment.

The incremental dumper is called in by the operating system at a time interval controlled by the installation manager (say every half hour) or as made necessary by shortage of space due to user file or expansion demands on the direct access backing store used by the operating system for file storage.

7.6.2 File Store Routine

This performs a complementary process to that of the incremental dumper: it finds a file or files previously dumped by the dumper. The system calls it in following machine breakdown, or when it receives a user program demand for a file which has been dumped out due to space shortage.

If after a machine breakdown the recovery procedure of GEORGE 3 discovers that some of the file store disc has been corrupted, then the file store routine is entered to scan through the increment magnetic tapes in reverse order of their creation and to recover the files residing on the part of the disc which has been corrupted. As soon as all the files being used by at least one active program have been recovered that program is reactivated. However, a longer pause may be necessary if the master directory is lost, since this must be reinstated before any program can be obeyed.

The other reason for entering the file store routine is to satisfy the requirements of a program which is demanding access to a file previously dumped to backing store due to lack of space on the operating system's disc. The operating system will try to batch up several requests. The file store routine then searches only the necessary increment tapes and restores to disc all needed files on each of them in turn.

7.6.3 Dump Processor

This is called in to rationalise the complete set of increment tapes. The frequency of its invocation is under the control of the installation manager. It extracts the latest versions of dumped files on to (usually) a smaller number of tapes and updates the increment index accordingly.

8

MULTIPLE ON-LINE PROCESSING LANGUAGES—CONVERSATIONAL MODE

DAVID FOSTER

In Chapter 5 the discussion on Multiaccess introduced the idea of conversational compilers. David Foster pursues this in greater depth, starting by describing the problems of communication with the user and his need for ready access to the machine. These are particularly relevant to program development and David Foster considers this in greater detail. He reviews the techniques used in the past to show the kind of facilities which would be desirable, and thus demonstrates the need for interaction. He then describes the development of conversational compilers to meet this need, and illustrates this by one such language available under GEORGE 3, JEAN. Finally, he shows how the benefits of such compilers can also be combined with those of more conventional languages, and illustrates this by a description of a conversational Fortran system.

8.1 The Communication Problem

One of the main factors on which the usefulness of a computer depends is the ease with which a user can tell it what he wants it to do. A computer can basically only perform very elementary operations such as adding two numbers together or comparing them for equality, and so for a computer to be able to solve a problem it must be expressed in terms of these basic operations. In fact a problem might require many thousands of such operations to define it and breaking the problem down into these operations would be a considerable task. From the user's point of view this is not the ideal way of instructing the computer how to solve his problem.

It is for this reason that programming languages and their associated compilers have been developed. The user can express his problem much more naturally in one of these languages. A special program known as a compiler is used to translate the problem from this language into the basic operations which the machine can perform. Using other terms we say that the compiler compiles from the source program, written in the programming language, into the object program, consisting of machine instructions.

Some such programming languages are COBOL, which permits programs for commercial applications to be written in a restricted form of English, ALGOL and FORTRAN based on standard mathematical notation, for scientific problems, and PL/I, which has been designed to cater for the needs of both commercial and scientific users. For example, the compiler can be instructed to calculate a root of the quadratic equation $Ax^2+Bx+C=O$ by the FORTRAN source statement

```
ROOT=(SQRT(B*B-4.0*A*C)-B)/(2.0*A)
```

It is clearly far simpler to give this statement to the computer than the 30 or so machine instructions describing the basic operations that would be necessary to perform this calculation.

8.2 The Access Problem

Programming languages go a long way towards solving the problem of communicating with a computer. However, there is another serious problem, that of access.

The most usual way in which people have been using computers has been by means of batch processing. The user writes his source program in a language such as ALGOL, COBOL or FORTRAN, gets it punched on cards or paper tape and then sends it off to the computer. It will be compiled, the object program executed and sometime later the results will be returned. It is probable that at first there will be errors in the program. The results will generally include some diagnostic information designed to help the user to find his mistakes, but it will, nevertheless, take a number of attempts and a period of time, before the program is working.

The critical factor in all this is the time between job submission and the return of the results. This will depend on a number of things such as the distance of the user's office from the machine, the load on the machine and the efficiency of the administrative system. If the work load is light and the user is close enough to the computer to be able to take his job there himself he might get it back within an hour. If his office is a long way from the machine and the work load is heavy the turnround time might be 24 or 48 hours.

In order that the user can get on with his work, what he really requires is immediate access to the computer. On way in which this can be provided is by a system such as WATFOR, an extremely fast FORTRAN batch load-and-go system developed at the University of Waterloo in Canada. This provides an almost cafeteria-like service to the student user who wants to compile and run a small FORTRAN job. The user queues to hand in his source program, punched on cards, to an operator who batches it with other programs and feeds it into a card reader. The queue then continues to a line printer where the user is able to take away his results immediately after they are printed. The queue then returns to the area of the card reader where the user is able to reclaim his cards. In practice there might be about 10 people waiting in the queue to hand in their cards to the operator, and the time between a user joining the queue and retrieving his cards might be about 2 minutes.

However, this service is limited in that it will only handle small programs in a restricted environment. The need for immediate access is more comprehensively met by the multiple on-line facilities provided by a system such as George 3. By means of a console typewriter near to or in his office and connected to the computer, the user can initiate and control the running of jobs remotely, instead of having to send them physically to the machine.

In particular he may have a FORTRAN or ALGOL program stored in a file in the file store. Using his console typewriter he can at any time call on the computer to compile and run this program. He can make use of any peripherals on the machine, but during the debugging of a program he will usually ask for his results to be typed on his typewriter and so avoid having to wait for them to be returned to him. If an error in his program is evident, he can at once edit his source program from his typewriter and recompile and run it. And so debugging of a program can proceed unhindered by frustrating turn-round delays.

8.3 The Need for Interaction

Another problem remains which is particularly important during the debugging of a program. As yet there is no real interaction between the user and the computer while the program is being compiled and run. First the user specifies what is to be done. Then the machine performs and returns the results and the user starts planning the next run. This is acceptable, but the user might be able to proceed much more quickly if there could be some interaction between the computer and the man.

In the early days of computers a user would sit at the control desk and monopolise the machine for a considerable time while he debugged his program in an interactive mode. He would stop at certain points and examine the contents of the store and then possibly amend the stored program and continue from where he left off. This is not done today because it is grossly inefficient for one man to have the machine to himself in this way and, moreover, it is better to communicate in terms of FORTRAN or ALGOL rather than in terms of the binary patterns stored in the machine. But in some respects it would be advantageous if, without the expensive inefficiency of the above practice, this kind of interactive facility were available.

For example, the following kind of facilities would be useful if they could be provided via the user's console typewriter.

1. When the user types in source statements on his typewriter, he is told immediately if there is a syntax error and is able to retype the statement.
2. Comprehensive error checking can be performed at execution time and when any error is detected the execution can be halted and the user informed.
3. On such halts or at pre-arranged stop points the user is able to examine the store by asking for specified variables to be typed out.
4. On such halts he is also able to reset the values of variables or modify the program by amending source statements before proceeding with the execution.

It was to provide these kinds of facilities that conversational languages were developed.

8.4 Conversational Language Systems

Conversational languages are similar to other languages such as ALGOL and FORTRAN in that they are designed to allow the user to express his problem to a computer in a natural way. But in addition they are designed for operation from a console typewriter and to allow the kinds of facilities listed above to be incorporated.

One of the first conversational languages to be developed was JOSS, written by J. C. Shaw of the RAND Corporation. The ICL conversational language JEAN developed for the 1900 series was based on JOSS and is very similar to it. These languages are designed to give the user the facilities he needs to develop and run conversationally programs to solve mathematical problems. They are also very simple and easy to learn.

At this point it is necessary to ask whether having a user operating his program in an interactive mode is an efficient way of using the computer. At first sight a user sitting at his console typewriter thinking about what corrective or diagnostic action to take next does not seem to make for efficiency.

However, the efficiency of such a system depends basically on timesharing. A large number of users can be using the system at the same time and when some users are sitting and thinking, or typing in on the typewriter, the computer can be occupied executing the programs of others. In most cases it is also possible for batch background jobs to be proceeding at the same time.

Also many conversational languages are, like JEAN, implemented in an incremental manner. This means that each statement of the source program is dealt with independently of the others until the time when execution takes place. If a statement is inserted or amended only that statement is affected and the whole program, or even a part of the program, does not have to be recompiled.

This is achieved in JEAN and some other systems by means of

interpretation. As the source statements are input they are not compiled immediately but are stored as a string of characters with very little processing. The string is interpreted when the statement is executed. This means slow execution but fast amendments, and when developing a program the time it takes to make amendments is probably the more important factor.

Other systems have increased their efficiency by processing the statements to a greater or lesser extent as they ate input, while still remaining incremental. This increases the execution speed while retaining the fast amendments feature.

8.5 JEAN

The JEAN system as implemented on the 1900 series allows a number of users (depending on the size of the machine) to construct and run simultaneously scientific and mathematical programs using console typewriters remote from the machine.

As in the Multiple On-line Processing facilities of GEORGE 3 (MOP) the user must wait until the symbol ← is typed out by the system as an invitation to type. The simplest thing he can then do is to type in a simple command to perform an arithmetic operation or sequence of operations and to type out the result or results. E.g.

```
←TYPE (79.15+33.27-15.3)*4
  (79.15+33.27-15.3)*4=388.48
←TYPE X*(X+1) FOR X=1(1)4
       X*(X+1)=          2
       X*(X+1)=          6
       X*(X+1)=         12
       X*(X+1)=         20
```

The second command causes the expression X*(X+1) to be evaluated four times with X taking values, 1, 2, 3, 4 sequentially.

Usually JEAN will be used to construct programs to perform more lengthy calculations consisting of several steps. To do this the indirect command is used. Each such command is preceded by a step number which is a mixed decimal number and irrespective of the order in which the steps are input they are performed in ascending numeric order of step number.

For example, a user could construct a program to calculate and type out the roots of the quadratic equation $Ax^2+Bx+C=O$ as follows:

```
←1.1 DEMAND A, B, C
←1.2 X=(-B+SQRT(B↑2-4*A*C))/(2*A)
←1.3 Y=(-B-SQRT(B↑2-4*A*C))/(2*A)
←1.4 TYPE X, Y IN FORM 1
←1.5 TO STEP 1.1
←FORM 1:
  ROOTS=###.###,###.###
```

When this program is executed, step 1.1 will cause a request for the values to be given to A, B and C to be typed out. After the user has typed in these values, steps 1.2 and 1.3 will calculate the roots. Then step 1.4 will cause them to be typed out in the specified format in which each occurrence of the symbol # represents a digit position. Step 1.5 causes a jump back to step 1.1 to take place and the process is then repeated.

The user may then decide to insert an instruction to halt the indefinite repetition of the process. He types

```
←1.1 DEMAND A
←1.13 DONE IF A=0
←1.16 DEMAND B, C
```

which causes the old step 1.1 to be replaced and two new steps to be inserted before step 1.2. The program will be halted if the value zero is given to A in response to the demand.

To cause the program to be executed the user types

```
←DO PART 1
```

This instructs the system to execute in order all the steps the integer part of whose numbers is 1. The following could be the resulting conversation

```
←DO PART 1
           A=←1
           B=←1
           C=←-12
 ROOTS=    3.000, -4.000
           A=←3
           B=←11
           C=←8
 ROOTS=    -1.000, -2.667
           A=←0
←
```

There are a number of interactive features in JEAN. Errors in syntax are discovered either immediately after a command has been input or when it is being obeyed. In either case the response is EH? and the user is able to re-input the corrected command. E.g.

```
←3.1 TIPE X, Y
  EH?
←3.1 TYPE X, Y
```

If an attempt is made to use a variable before a value has been set to it, JEAN will inform the user of this. E.g. if the variable is Z, JEAN will type a message such as

```
INTERRUPTED: Z=???
←
```

The user may then set a value to Z and continue.

Other semantic errors cause an appropriate message to be typed out and a halt in the execution to take place. At such halts, and also at prearranged halts, the user can have values of variables typed out by using the TYPE command. He can also modify his program by re-inputting or inserting steps and resume it at any specified point. E.g.

```
←2.4 Z=(Y-1)*(Y-2)-1
←2.5 X=X/(1-Z↑2)
      .
      .
      .
      .
      .
←DO PART 2
  ERROR AT STEP 2.5: I HAVE A ZERO DIVISOR
←TYPE Y, Z
             Y=  3
             Z=  1
←2.45 Z=Z/4
←TO STEP 2.45
```

Here the user was able to insert the instruction he had previously omitted and re-enter the program at that point.

8.6 The Position of Conventional Languages

A system such as JEAN offers several advantages to the user. Its main strength lies in its interactive and conversational facilities. Such facilities make it possible for a user to develop a program easily and in the shortest possible time.

Moreover JEAN is implemented by an incremental and interpretive system. As we have seen this means slow execution, but it also means fast amendments which is an asset for development work.

However, a conventional compiling system such as FORTRAN offers several advantages over JEAN. The user has a more powerful language available and so he can more sensibly construct larger and more complex programs. Also FORTRAN is a well established international language. Many FORTRAN programs and subroutines exist and are readily available for use. Furthermore, although the debugging of a FORTRAN program may take longer than the debugging of a similar program in JEAN, once the program is working the FORTRAN compiler will normally leave the user with a fairly efficient object program. If it is then necessary to run the debugged program a large number of times, it will certainly be more costly in machine time to run it under a system such as JEAN than to run the compiled FORTRAN program.

It was therefore a natural next step to try to combine the advantages of both types of system by the development of conversational compilers for conventional languages and many computer manufacturers and users have done or are doing this.

A notable example of such a conversational system is the RUSH system developed by Allen-Babcock Computing, Inc. This system, which is based on the PL/I language, is the basis for a remote access computing service. At the time of writing there are about 150 terminals attached to their computer to service users from all over the United States.

A number of requirements of a conversational system for a language such as FORTRAN can be listed.

1. It should be possible to input, compile, debug and execute a program entirely from a remote console typewriter, although it should be permissible to make use of other peripherals if required.
2. The emphasis should be on quick and easy debugging. Comprehensive diagnostic aids should be provided, and especially the interactive facilities listed in Section 8.3 'The Need for Interaction'.
3. It should be possible to make amendments quickly and easily and without lengthy recompilations being required.
   It should also be possible to make at least minor amendments when execution has been halted in the middle of a program, and then to continue the execution without having to start it again at the beginning.
4. The speed of execution of the user's program should be as fast as possible within the constraints set by requirements 2 and 3. In addition, having debugged a program conversationally it should be possible to compile it automatically into an efficient object program.
5. It should be possible for the system to be used efficiently by a large number of users at the same time.

These requirements are the chief ones that have been borne in mind during the design of the ICL 1900 FORTRAN Conversational System and the following section gives an indication of some of the facilities it includes.

8.7 The ICL 1900 FORTRAN Conversational System

The system is designed to allow a user to develop a FORTRAN program from a console typewriter. It is based on units of FORTRAN statements and FORTRAN segments. Within a segment each statement has associated with it a unique line number which is a mixed decimal number.

As in JEAN, the user has to wait until the symbol ← is output as an invitation to type, before he types anything himself.

In order to construct a segment the user must first type a segment statement in response to the invitation to type. The system responds by typing the name of the segment enclosed in parentheses at the left-hand end of the next line, to indicate that this segment is now what is known as the current segment. It will then type the line number 1 on the next line, followed by ←, inviting the user to type in the first statement. When the user has typed in this statement he will be invited to type in the next and so on. To end the segment he must type in END as his response. E.g.

```
←REAL FUNCTION AREA (A, B, C)
 (AREA)
   1←S=(A+B+C)
   2←AREA=SQRT(S*(S-A)*(S-B)*(S-C))
   3←END
←
```

To replace or insert a statement in the current segment, all the user has to do is to type in the line number of this statement, followed by the new statement itself. E.g.

```
←1 S=(A+B+C)/2.0
←55.5 RETURN
```

The user could then cause the amended segment to be listed. His command, and the response, would be

```
←LIST AREA
  0 REAL FUNCTION AREA (A, B, C)
  1     S=(A+B+C)/2.0
  2     AREA
 55.5   RETURN
       END
```

The rather exotic choice of line number for the RETURN illustrates how segments can be extended. It should also be noted that if the user wishes to construct the inner parts of his segment first, rather than to type in his segment from the beginning, he can do this by first constructing an empty segment and then using the editing facilities.

Facilities are also included to allow users to delete statements, or to replace or insert blocks of statements or to copy them from one segment to another.

When a line of source program is presented to the system, its syntax is checked. If an error is discovered the response EH? is typed on the next line. The user is then given an opportunity to retype the statement.

At this point, if the user requires further information about an error, this can be obtained by typing HELP. After this information has been given, the user will again be able to re-type the statement. E.g.

```
  33←A=(X+1/(X+1/(X+1/(X+1/X)))
EH?
  33←HELP
```

```
MISSING PARENTHESIS
   33←A=(X+1/(X+1/(X+1/(X+1/X))))
   34←
```

Various trace facilities are provided to allow the user to find out what is happening as his program is executed. He is able to specify diagnostic printing indicating the transfers of control that take place, or the printing of intermediate results. He is also able to specify halts at chosen points in the program.

Execution of the user's program can be initiated by means of the directive

```
←RUN
```

Execution might be halted for one of several reasons. For example, a STOP instruction might be encountered, a halt point specified by the user might be reached, or an error diagnosed. In each case an appropriate message will be typed out indicating what has happened and at what statement in the program the halt has occurred.

On such halts there are a number of actions the user can take. He may list part of his program, or amend it, or modify the diagnostic printing being produced. He may cause the values of specified variables, array elements, etc. to be printed out. He may type a single FORTRAN statement without preceding it with a line number. In this case the statement will not be stored but will be executed immediately and by this means the user can, for example, reset the value of a variable or GO TO a labelled statement. He may then, in most cases, follow such actions by typing

```
←GO
```

which causes the execution to continue from the point of the halt. This will not, however, be possible if he has made the sort of amendments, e.g. changing the type of variables, that would necessitate execution starting again at the beginning.

The user will also be able to interrupt his program at any time, which he may want to do if he suspects his program is looping. He will then be able to take the same kind of actions as were available to him at halts.

The output produced during the execution of a program normally comes out on the user's console typewriter, and input required is requested from the user as it is needed. However, it is possible for the user to construct segments of data and so set up the input required in advance of the execution. Such data segments can be edited.

The system is designed to work under GEORGE 3 or GEORGE 4 and so the user can specify as an alternative that the input is to be taken from a file in the file store, or output sent to one. Similarly the program source may be taken from, and listings sent to, such a file.

The system works incrementally. Executable statements are compiled without reference to the effects of declarations, and the declarations cause tables to be set up. When execution is initiated by a RUN directive, the compiled program is first scanned and 'fixed up' according to the declarations.

The statements are compiled into blocks of instructions joined together in a list structure. Hence it is possible to insert and delete statements without recompilation being necessary, and normally it is possible to continue execution after an amendment from the point at which it was interrupted. If a declaration is amended it is then necessary to go back to re-scan and fix up the program, but full recompilation is not necessary. Hence amendments can be implemented quickly.

Because of the nature of the object program, the execution speed may be about three times slower than it would be for code generated by a conventional compiler. This is, however, acceptable for development runs and once a program is working it will be possible to call in a conventional compiler to compile it efficiently. Moreover, it will be possible to compile developed subroutines in this way and then interface these subroutines with the program being developed interactively.

As the system is designed to run under GEORGE 3 it is the Operating System that will arrange that a number of users can use it at the same time. The system will be most useful working on a paged machine such as the 1906A, using the paged version of the Operating System, GEORGE 4. In this case a large virtual store will be available and it will be possible for a large number of users to share one copy of the conversational system in the store, but for each to have his own area of working store. Transfers to and from backing store will only take place if necessary and it is likely that the conversational system itself will always remain in core.

9

REAL TIME—SPECIAL REQUIREMENTS FOR CONTROL SOFTWARE

STUART J. MILLER

Through Executive and the Georges we have been able to illustrate most of the facilities contained in batch and multiaccess operating systems. To find out about real time we leave this family, and Stuart Miller chooses the Univac STARS system for this purpose. First he describes the characteristics of real time, and in particular explains why it needs different software concepts to Batch processing. He then discusses and illustrates the type of control system required, the means for handling the complex communications networks required, and the special problems associated with random access equipment in such an environment. Finally, after considering the control of programs and timing, he discusses the important issue of speedy recovery after failure.

9.1 Introduction

The many features of conventional batch processing are today well-known to most people who have any contact with computers. Over the years of computer development there has always been the aim of greater efficiency and throughput for such systems, and this led initially to faster stores and hardware logic together with architectural changes, soon followed by the ability of a single computer to perform several tasks concurrently. This latter development could only have been achieved by greater cooperation between software and hardware designers that had been usual previously. As a result of these and other improvements, great attention has been paid to the benefits derived from installing computers in commercial, governmental, academic and utility environments. Claims made by users about the performance of their computers have become increasingly impressive.

Development of computer systems—that is to say, the interaction of computer and environment—continues apace with other developments. The branch which assuredly has an increasing effect upon the applications of computers is that of *Real Time Computer Systems*.

To understand what is meant by the term *Real Time*, it is necessary first to recognise the conceptual structure of any organisation. An organisation's operation consists of a set of procedures, whether it is the production of shafts on a lathe, the updating of financial accounts or decision-making in the boardroom. This applies equally well to commercial, governmental, academic and utility organisations. The degree of human participation varies with the different procedures. Thus, the role of a man who supervises a bottling machine may be considered more passive than active, whereas the converse is true for, say, a bank cashier. Any procedure can be broken down into elements, which can be called subsets of the main procedure, and this fractionalising can be continued indefinitely. It is now possible to return to the premise and state that a hierarchy of interactive procedures constitutes an organisation.

This statement is not as esoteric as it sounds since it enables the principles of real time computing to be defined in general terms. Thus, a real time computer system is one in which computer and man combine in interactive partnership to perform a procedure, *where the interface between man and computer is determined solely by the requirements of the man.* In contrast to this definition, it is clear that the interface between man and computer in a conventional batch system is determined by the computer's requirements.

Historically, there are three basic types of real time computer system:

1. *Process control systems*

   Where human participation in the procedures is more passive than active; also where environmental performance requirements are most stringent. These systems are normally applied to industrial processes but include such applications as traffic control systems and space flight monitoring.

2. *Commercial Real time systems*

   Where the interaction between man and computer is at its highest, each partner performing different elements of a procedure, making decisions and reacting. They are typically used for airline reservations, medical applications, banks, information systems and others which may be considered central file oriented.

3. *Multiaccess systems*

   Where several users share the computer, each for an independent purpose. Currently, these are used in academic, scientific and some commercial environments.

In this chapter we are concerned with commercial real time systems—those which may be called *multi-user job systems*, as distinct from multiaccess systems which may be called *multi-job user systems*. The software aspects of process control systems are more specialised and outside the scope of this book.

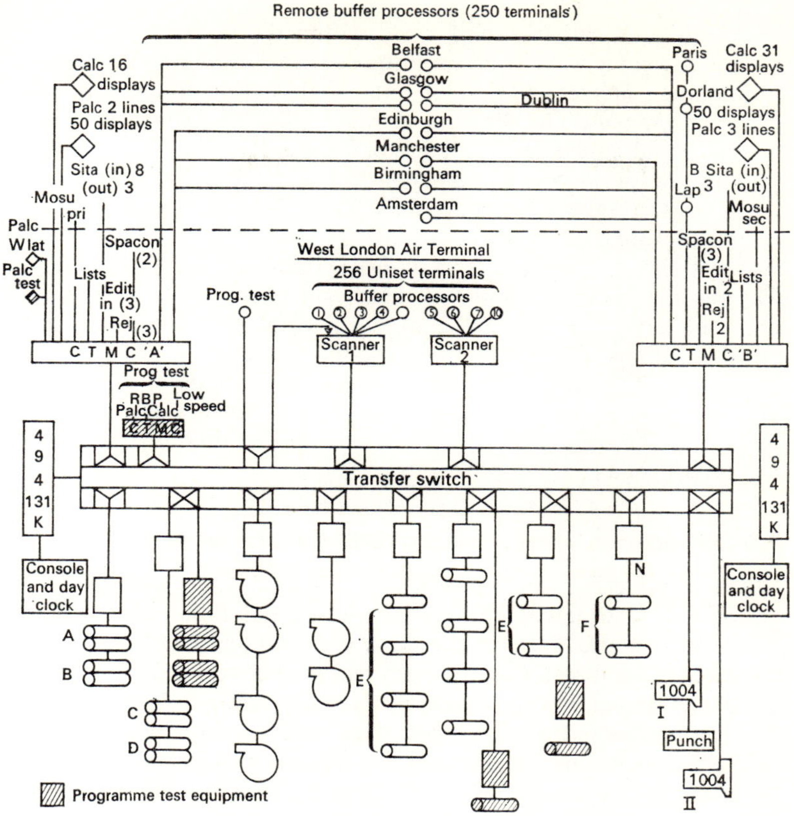

Fig. 13.

Fig. 13 shows a configuration for a typical large commercial real time system. The most important hardware aspects of such a system are:

1. *Emphasis on communications equipment*
   Although a complete communications network is not shown it will be clearly understood that its complexity will be large owing to the number of users and their wide geographical placement. Multiplexers may be cascaded and there will usually be remote buffering control units.
2. *Duplication of equipment*
   Since the system is dedicated to the needs of the human user, interruptions to service should be as limited as possible. Both software and hardware are fallible and when a breakdown occurs there must be alternative equipment to continue with the service. The duplication applies to central processors, file and communications equipment.

3. *Large file stores*

Nearly all activities performed within the system concern the files in some way. Their importance is such that security is paramount; any corruption of data could create havoc with the environment. The diagram shows duplicated main files (AB=CD) and duplicated small files or indexes (E=F). These are held on random access equipment which also hold the system programs. Magnetic tapes are used for periodic file dumps and for background batch work.

At any point in time there is an *on-line* system and an *off-line* system. The on-line system contains all hardware necessary to handle the real time service, i.e. one CPU, all four multiplexers, files AB, CD, E and F, one tape channel and one channel devoted to card the print operations. The off-line system consists of the remaining equipment and at this stage may be doing conventional batch work, program testing etc. Transfer switches will be provided so that any peripheral can be switched to either processor.

9.2 Differences in software concepts between batch and real-time

When considering control software for real time systems it is essential first to recognise a basic functional difference between these systems and those of the more conventional batch variety. It has already been seen that the term real time covers a wide range of computer system, but for the purposes of this paragraph at least they may be considered as like types, each of them having a common functional aspect in that the majority of activities in the system are initiated by some external event. This is the exact converse of a batch system where the majority of activities emanate from some internal event (usually as a result of some program command). It is convenient to call real time systems *exogenous*, and batch systems *endogenous*. In order to clarify this point consider a simple program which has been written to update records in a file according to items of input data. In a batch environment this program would handle each item of input data and only when completed would it call for the next item and repeat the process until the data stream is exhausted (this is true even if the program employs double or multiple buffering techniques). The activation of each item of processing is thus at the complete discretion of the program.

Now consider this same program in a real time environment where, because the input data items come from terminals operated by humans—notoriously unpredictable—it would be inefficient to adopt similar tactics since the program would then be funnelling these items and only dealing with them in a serial fashion, thus delaying the human operators during periods of peak activity (this can be emphasised by queuing theory or by a large supermarket on a

Saturday morning with only one cash point). If the terminals were in fact analogue monitoring points in, say, a steel rolling mill or a chemical plant, any delays could very easily lead to chaos or even catastrophe. In spite of this exogenous facet of real time systems it is necessary that the central computer should at all times be in control of its own status; one of the duties of a control system in this environment is to accept exogenous events in an endogenous fashion (see 9.4, 'Communications') and ensure that processing is delayed as little as possible.

Any event which occurs within the system can be considered as a request to perform a task. The event could be an interrupt from the communications equipment or from the files, or a request from an application program to the control system. In order to satisfy these requirements the control system will have to deploy resources on this task. In this sense, program coding, processor store and processor time can be considered as resources. There will be many simultaneous calls on these resources and the control system has the responsibility of optimising their deployment so that delays to task processing are as small as possible. Priorities will be applied to every possible event and the initiation of associated activities will depend upon these priorities.

9.3 Structure of the Control System

The hub of the control system consists of a program loop which detects the occurrence of any event (by means of program switches) and schedules the appropriate resources to handle it. This loop is variously called the *schedule scan*, *priority scan*, *switcher*, *dynamic allocator*, *control exchange* or *idling loop*. All the event switches are inspected in a strict priority sequence and if nothing has occurred by the time the end is reached, the scan is recycled. The priority sequence varies with different systems and is determined according to system design considerations which will show certain activities as being more time critical than others. In general it is true to say that peripheral interrupts carry the highest priority since their occurrence implies a change in the status of the system. Also, hardware constraints may mean that an action is required on that peripheral within a certain time period for it to continue functioning correctly. Worker programs which await use of the central processor will be placed low in the scan owing to the fact that all essential system tasks must be performed first. The overall aim in deciding the priority sequence will be to minimise queue lengths at every point which is subject to the formation of a queue.

Fig. 14 shows the general scan sequence adopted by UNIVAC in their real time control system, STARS. This control system, developed from Eastern Airlines/UNIVAC CONTORTS, is imple-

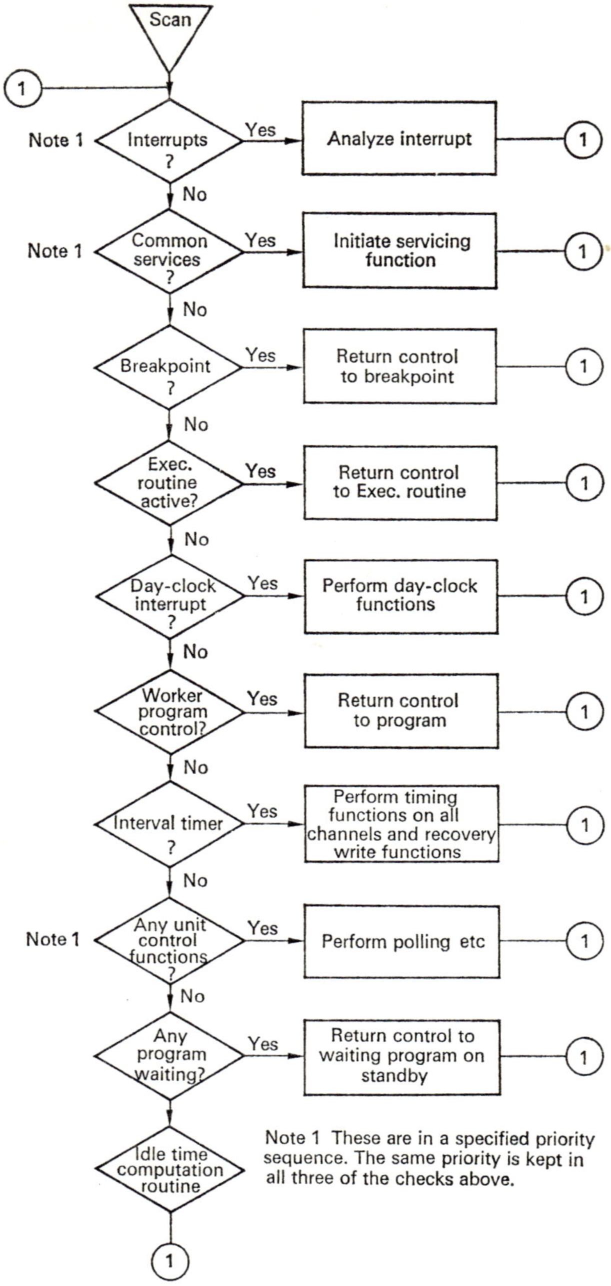
Scan
1
Note 1
Interrupts ?
Yes
Analyze interrupt
1
No
Note 1
Common services ?
Yes
Initiate servicing function
1
No
Breakpoint ?
Yes
Return control to breakpoint
1
No
Exec. routine active?
Yes
Return control to Exec. routine
1
No
Day-clock interrupt ?
Yes
Perform day-clock functions
1
No
Worker program control?
Yes
Return control to program
1
No
Interval timer ?
Yes
Perform timing functions on all channels and recovery write functions
1
No
Note 1
Any unit control functions ?
Yes
Perform polling etc
1
No
Any program waiting?
Yes
Return control to waiting program on standby
1
Idle time computation routine
Note 1 These are in a specified priority sequence. The same priority is kept in all three of the checks above.
1

Fig. 14.

mented on UNIVAC 494 computer systems. At British European Airways it is responsible for the control of some 200 000 transactions daily from over 600 terminal sets. These terminals are sited throughout Europe and the transactions may concern reservations, passenger handling, cargo handling, aircraft weight and balance and so on. Each transaction makes several references to the files held on drums and exists in the computer for nearly a ½-second on average. The majority of this existence time is taken up with queuing for various resources and if the scan is in any way inefficient, the queues would increase and the existence time would rise exponentially. This would cause the responses to the terminals to be seriously delayed with consequent hold-ups in the airline's operation. It will be seen that apart from inspecting event switches the STARS schedule scan performs a timing function on peripheral and other actions (as distinct from hardware timers), and also monitors utilisation of the central processor.

There are basically three types of task which such a real time system has to perform:

1. Peripheral control tasks
2. Transaction processing tasks
3. System maintenance and control tasks

The first and last of these are performed mostly by the control system; the second is performed by worker programs which handle all processing of transactions. Routines exist which are driven by exits from the schedule scan according to associated switches.

Examples under the three headings above are:

1. Communications handlers, drum/disc handlers, magnetic tape handlers, card/print handlers.
2. Reservations processing, message switching, passenger check-in etc.
3. Resource allocation, program scheduling, recovery control, time-based activities.

For transaction processing tasks, a similar priority structure is defined for central processor control with queues organised at each priority level. The levels are shown in Fig. 15. When one of these tasks is ready for control—after an input-output action, after being interrupted or at initiation—it is added to the appropriate queue and the switch set in the schedule scan. When this switch is detected, the worker program queues are inspected and the highest priority task is given control. An important aspect is that when a task has been completed—or has reached a convenient check point—the schedule scan is entered at the beginning so that the priorities of other waiting tasks can be respected.

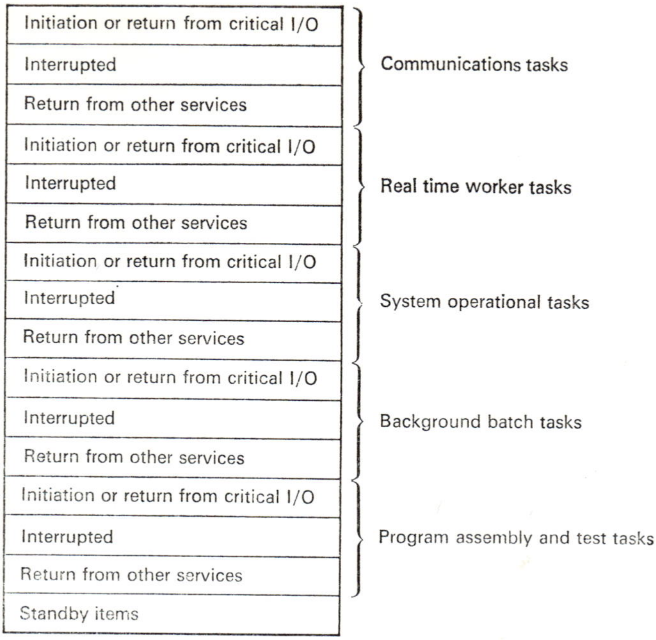

Fig. 15.

9.4 Communications Handling

It has already been seen that in large real time systems the communications networks are very complex. One network may contain different terminal devices and remote buffering control units, different modes and speeds of transmission, different character codes and polling strategies, all of which contribute to this complexity. In terms of control software it is thus difficult to provide generalised handlers. Many software executives which purport to have real time capability tend to organise the communications aspect as an appendage to the main structure, which implies a certain incoherence in the general flow of control. In general it is desirable that the framework of the control system be built around the communications handling task since, in the last analysis, it is only that task which can control the overall level of activity in the system.

The main task of the communications handler (CH) is to provide a second-level smoothing operation on the peaks and troughs of demand on the system. The first level of smoothing will be performed by the remote buffering control units, if any. Although, as we have seen, the nature of a real time system is exogenous it would not normally be possible to permit messages for processing to arrive at the central processor without some reference to its existing status of workload. The CH will employ a 'polling' system which means that it will ask a remote device for a message. Without this poll, no messages can be despatched to the central processor. Thus, if the workload in the central system is very heavy at a particular instant in time the CH will not poll for any more messages. Some networks use a system of 'status polling', where the message poll is preceded by a request from the CH to the device saying: 'do you have any messages?'—the reply to this being merely 'yes' or 'no'. This allows the CH to build up a picture of the imminent workload on the system before requesting messages, but it can be expensive in terms of line utilisation. Different conditions exist where there are several controlling devices on one line. In some cases, a poll is sent to one of the devices which itself polls the next, tagging its message to the end, and so on; the last device transmits back to the central processor. In others, the devices are polled individually in a cyclic fashion, or according to their own workload status.

Another aspect of input is that lesser priority messages may be 'staged' on drums or discs. This means that the messages which arrive at the central processor are immediately written away to backing store before being processed. With this method it is possible to provide a third-level smoothing operation.

Whatever method is chosen for handling input, consideration is always given to the effects on overall response time, message queue lengths, line utilisation, failure and recovery aspects and overload situations.

As far as message output is concerned, the transaction processing program normally supplies the terminal identifier with the message, which is then transmitted by the CH. Again, different techniques are employed. The STARS system mentioned above will stage some output messages whilst transmitting others directly. Consideration will of course be given to the lines being duplex or half-duplex.

9.5 Random access equipment handling

The distinguishing features of files in a real time system are first that there will be many concurrent users of the same files, and second that many of the files will be dynamically volatile. This latter distinction means that the overall file size varies constantly as transactions create and delete records. As the need arises to create a new record, space must be found on the file and so 'free-space' control techniques must be employed.

The majority of transaction existence time in commercial real time systems is taken up by file accesses—around two million accesses are made daily on the B.E.A. system—and every method possible has to be used to minimise this time. This is done initially by careful selection of hardware and by efficient file design. There is frequently a great temptation to design multi-level tree-structured files which facilitate the eventual addressing of the records, but compromises have to be made in order to reduce the number of necessary accesses. Frequently used indexes, if too big to maintain in core store, should be held on fast access drums with fixed read/write heads if possible; less used records can be held on slower, moving head devices. The random access handler (RAH) should be responsible for optimising head movement on the big devices since this takes most of the time.

A further compromise has to be made between the amount of data security and integrity checks performed by the worker programs and the RAH. There is a limit for these checks beyond which response times may be seriously affected. There is also another limit below which the files will become very vulnerable to corruption.

One possibility of corruption is that two transactions may concurrently require access to the same record. If this were allowed to happen, different amendments would be made to that record, with the result that one of them would be overwritten. The RAH will provide a request facility which says: 'read record x and inhibit its use by any other program.' There will also be a converse facility which says: 'release record x for general use.' In certain cases the need arises for a complete file to have a temporary lockout, such as when it may be undergoing a repacking exercise, but this will be restricted to infrequently used files or the general real time system will be shut down during that period.

It has already been seen that duplicate files will often be maintained for the purposes of security. If these files are on separate input-output channels a time benefit is also gained. The maintenance of duplicate files means that read accesses can be performed from either channel whereas write accesses must be made to both. Reference to queuing theory will show that if the proportion of reads to writes is 50 per cent or more a decrease in mean queue length will be realised over a single channel. Naturally, the RAH arranges for the simultaneous update of both file copies. When hardware is required for routine maintenance there will still be another copy in use to continue with the real time operation, albeit at a reduced level of security. The control system will be responsible for reconstituting data on the second copy when it is returned; this will be done without stopping the system.

Another method of security often used is that all file updates are copied to another unit—either random access or magnetic tape. If a unit failure occurs, the data can then be reconstituted by updating a previous file dump with this 'journal'. This of course takes time.

9.6 Control of worker programs and resource allocation

When a message arrives at the central processor it requires several resources before it can be processed. It needs core space for itself and for buffers which will be used as work area and to contain associated records, and it needs processor control time in order to obey the worker program coding. The requirements for file accesses have been dealt with in the previous paragraph.

It is frequently the case that several messages of the same type will require the same coding concurrently. In order to avoid having several copies of this coding in core at the same time, a technique known as *re-entrant coding* is often employed by the worker programs. Re-entrant programs allow timesharing between transactions instead of sequential processing, without the need to maintain several copies of the programs in the core memory. The effect of such timesharing in applications which are basically input-output limited is to maintain a queue of input-output requests, particularly for the vital random access storage channels. With an efficient control system, delay between input-output operations at busy times may thus be minimised. One requirement for this technique is that all work areas pertaining to a particular transaction should be separate from the coding and unique to the transaction. Thus, when control is removed temporarily from a transaction by the control software, contents of all registers should be preserved in the unique area.

The control software has the responsibility of allocating the necessary work areas required and for preserving the integrity of data contained therein. Most contemporary computers have a system of core protection which prevents any one transaction from trespassing on to another's buffers, but this protection becomes complex when considering the dynamic allocation of core store. The most efficient method of allocating this store is for the control system to have an algorithm which will donate areas of any size from a common store pool as they are required and return them to the pool when surrendered by the worker program. If uncontrolled, this method can lead to fragmentation of the pool and usually implies that buffers for a particular transaction will not be in a contiguous area, but the alternative of allocating fixed size areas is wasteful. The worker programs will always address their buffers via index registers and so they must be informed of the buffer base address when being given its use.

Many worker programs will be partitioned such that segments are loaded into core from drum only as they are required. The control system should provide a facility such that when a request for a segment is received, either that task is queued, if the segment is re-entrant and already in core, or the segment is loaded into an appropriate place and activated. It is preferable for the segment to be loaded into any area large enough.

9.7 Timer activities

The time element is clearly very important in a real time system. It is always necessary for the system to maintain an awareness of ambient time, relating it to internal activities. Some form of reference clock will be provided by hardware—very often several clocks which provide a time of day reading as well as strict interval interrupts. These check points will be used by the control system for two basic purposes. Firstly, to schedule certain tasks which need to be performed at a specific time of day, and secondly to provide a fine time check on all system activities for monitoring purposes.

There are many programs of the batch variety which may need to run at specific times of the day. Examples of these are file dumps, file purges and file scans. Rather than rely on operators to call these programs at the correct time (even a few seconds error may be critical) a list should be maintained by the control system, inspected every minute, say, and any appropriate programs called. It may also be a requirement that periodic displays of system utilisation are output to the console or printer for statistical purposes.

Owing to the special requirements of a commercial real time system it is not usually necessary for the control system to allocate 'time-slots' to programs run in the batch mode, unless they are excessively compute bound. The priority structure of worker program tasks shown in Fig. 15 (page 92) will ensure that real time transactions are not neglected. There will be a continuous stream of interrupts from external sources which will allow the control system to make due reference to priorities and prevent batch programs disrupting the normal flow of real time work. It is possible, however, that programs will fall into an eternal looping situation which, unless checked, could remain unobserved and maybe cause damage to data. In order to prevent these situations, each time it gets control the control system should check the maximum estimated running time of the program (supplied at program call-time as a parameter) against the actual running time. If it has been exceeded, either a close-out of the program will be enforced, or the operators will be notified, in case they wish to take alternative action. A maximum permissible compute time check between deliberate control system reference points could also be made as a further safeguard.

Control systems themselves are by no means infallible and time checks may also be made on their own internal activities. Most of these activities will be run in interruptable mode and if their time quota is exceeded, the operators will be informed, so as to investigate and restart the system.

When an item needs to be queued for a particular resource, the total time spent waiting may be monitored in order to guard against suspected bottlenecks. Statistics may be collected of the number of times a particular limit is exceeded so that systems designers can check on their original performance estimates. Peripheral actions should certainly be time checked since the sudden 'loss' of an on-line device might otherwise be undetected.

9.8 Failures and recovery

If a failure occurs in the hardware or software of a batch system, it is usually possible to restart the programs from a convenient checkpoint so that the only loss to the system is an overall time delay. Unfortunately in a real time system, the delay could be critical—apart from the disruption in service to the human users. The passage of time is inexorable and while the system is in a stopped condition some essential functions may be missed. Even more important, transactions may be only partially completed when failure occurs and unless rigid integrity checks are carried out after restart but before 'open-shop' condition is reached, there is a high probability that data records will be harmed by double updates or overwriting.

Both control software and applications programs have a responsibility towards system security and quick, efficient restart and recovery. The techniques used for this purpose vary with the needs of individual systems, but emphasis is always placed on the security of file data and the continuity of transactions. Other aspects which receive important consideration are information to the user, so that he knows when the system is 'down' (the lack of a response is not always sufficient evidence), instructions to the user to perform special actions on restart, if required, and diagnostic information to enable the fault to be traced.

With the plethora of interaction which exists in real time, it is important to detect a fault as soon as possible after its occurrence. Many hardware systems aid by interrupting on conditions such as core parity fail, power fluctuation, excessive lockout of interrupts, core protect violation, illegal instruction, clock overflow and so on. At such times the control system should ascertain the security of the condition and take appropriate remedial action. This may involve the temporary close-down of some or all real time operations whilst a tidying process is carried out, or even recording the status of the system prior to a complete, orderly shut-down. It has already been seen that larger systems will have duplicated hardware to allow a continuation of operation, but if the fault is recurrent and caused by software it will have to be traced before a restart can be made.

It is not always possible for the control software to record conditions within the system before stopping, so there must be frequent checkpoints during normal running to facilitate recovery. The UNIVAC STARS system writes control tables relating to file control and communications status onto two media at five second intervals, so that if a sudden failure occurs the amount of recovery work to be done is limited.

Upon bootstrap and restart of the system—performed either manually or by program action—all dynamic status information will be given careful confidence checks, hardware connections checked by software, remote buffering units informed of the failure, veracity of files checked, system control tables reconstructed, message continuity assured and programs called which were either running at fail time or should have run during the down period. When all this has been done by the control system, communications lines will be polled and real time operations restarted. The whole process will take less than a minute from fail time.

9.9 Conclusion

It will be clear that the main requirements for real time control software are:

1. Concentration on communications aspects
2. Volatile file handling
3. Efficient low-level scheduling
4. Time consciousness
5. Awareness of failures

It goes without saying that overheads involved in supervisory work should be as low as possible. This requirement means that many functions of a batch operating system would be onerous if applied to real time. Such facilities as high-level schedulers, jobstream languages, data cooperatives, complex file control techniques, conversational compilers, etc. would have debilitating effects on performance. With processor speeds now being very fast, however, and the requirements of computer users being more catholic, a convergence of operating systems is likely. Several attempts have already been made to produce universal operating systems but success has largely been elusive when applied to large scale systems.

10

THE J LEVEL SYSTEM

MARTIN WARWICK

With real time we have now covered all the major aspects of operating systems. But the illustrations used have been drawn from only one system in each case, and Martin Warwick enlarges the picture by describing the comparable system for another machine, System 4, which is typical of those having an architecture derived from IBM's 360 series. His description includes Supervisor, Data Management, Job Control and the Trials system, and by comparison with the systems of earlier chapters he demonstrates the wide variety of different techniques that have been developed to achieve the same basic ends. The manner in which Operating systems will progress in the future is left to the reader.

10.1 Introduction

In previous chapters the description of general purpose operating systems has been mainly related to those for the ICL 1900 Series. Every computer or at least every series has its own individual system, and in this chapter one designed for another range of machines is described by way of contrast.

In meeting the general requirements for an operating system, described earlier in the book, many factors influence the eventual product. Clearly the hardware influences the design and the philosophies of the methods of operation, but perhaps the most important single factor is the image of the average user. If the average job serviced is a large, long running data processing program then the systems overheads are relatively unimportant. The system can afford to be thorough and full of facilities. If, on the other hand, the average is a student job with a program of very short duration then the overheads are of very major concern and are likely to take a high proportion of the total capacity.

A system which specialises in a particular job type optimises its throughput for this use. The one described in this chapter can be termed a General Purpose Operating System in that it offers a cover to all types of job mix and offers facilities for all users without optimising on any one particular user image. It is from the same manufacturer ICL, but designed for the System 4 range. It is known as the J level Operating System and it operates on any of the larger models of the range (the 4-40, 4-50, 4-70). It is disc operating, that is it relies on the use of a disc, and in its basic form it requires a 65K byte main store (32 bits ≡ 4 bytes ≡ 1 word), 2 replaceable disc stores, a card reader and a line printer. This configuration can be extended by core store, fixed disc file, magnetic tapes, drums, and other peripheral devices including communications equipment.

To look at the system in more detail we will subdivide it in the following way:

The Supervisor

The Data Management System

Job Control

The Trials System

10.2 Differences from 1900 systems

One difference between J Level and the systems described in previous chapters is the absence of an Executive. Many of the functions that were contained in GEORGE 1, 2, 3 and those that were placed in the Executive are collected together in a single package known as Supervisor. This integrated package can claim as its advantage that its operations are single level while in an Executive plus Operating System complex some operations have to be performed twice, once to guarantee their integrity within the Operating System and secondly within the scope of the Executive. Counter arguments would concern the structure of a single program of this size—how monolithic is it?—how easy is it to understand and alter? In fact, due to its structure a great deal of modularity can be claimed. It consists of a great number of separate segments together with a central control and it is relatively simple to handle the separate facilities and insert new ones.

Any system has an internal structure which is the province of the designers and the implementors, and an external structure which is the view the user has of it. The internal structure and its efficiency are dependent to some degree on the hardware architecture. System 4 has a user code compatible with that of the IBM 360. Its privilege architecture, that is, the hardware interface which is hidden by the operating system, differs in many significant ways. There are four Processor States known as P1, P2, P3, P4. A Processor State defines a set of hardware registers; each State has its own set. After any instruction a program in one Processor State can be halted and another State can be entered without any change in the registers. The interrupt system is such that machine failure (power supply, internal parity) causes State P4 to be entered, and all other interrupts cause P3 to be entered. P1 and P2 are normal programming States and are used in the J level system for user programs and Supervisor routines respectively.

Another major difference between System 4 and the 1900 series lies in the control of peripheral devices. System 4, as with the IBM360, controls its input-output by means of Command Chains. Each input-output channel unit has the ability to interpret a chain or a series of commands which control the positioning of magnetic tapes, the positioning of disc heads, the transferring of data and other actions. It is possible, using these facilities, to have executed by the input-output channel a program of actions which will perform a set of operations on the peripheral and these actions are performed asynchronously with central processor execution. Very complex procedures are possible using Command Chains especially on random access devices which are formatted to make full use of these facilities. It rests upon the Operating System to enable these complexities to be fully utilised and yet to be transparent to the user.

10.3 The Supervisor

The four Processor States have already been mentioned. The Supervisor is entered from a machine interrupt when its coding in the P3 State is obeyed. This coding is known as the Kernel and is the central analysis routine for interrupts. As little work as is possible is performed in the Kernel although the most frequent causes for entering it, the basic input-output routines, are serviced entirely within it. The Kernel acts as the switching module and its basic task is to set up the conditions which cause other parts of the system to be entered. Its operation is short and this is necessary as it is the one part of the operating system which is not interruptable. When the Kernel has completed its operation it searches the list of jobs which are ready to run in the P1 or P2 states for the one of the highest priority and then causes it to be obeyed. The list of jobs, tasks, or routines, is known as the Routine Table.

The P1 jobs are mainly user supplied; the P2 routines are the tasks which create the Supervisor facilities. These are fully interruptable and apart from having privileges which are not available to the normal user, do not differ noticeably from user programs. Most important of all they can use the Supervisor facilities themselves and can call upon these facilities by the normal Supervisor Call.

The value of this Supervisor structure is immense, and the following four points emphasise its advantages and its strength.

1. The Kernel is the only monolithic or integrated part of the Operating System but it is small and of a manageable size.
2. All facilities of the system are separate modules apart from the Kernel.

3. Each routine is fully interruptable and hence can use the facilities of the Supervisor itself. When one routine wishes to use the facilities provided by another it calls upon it in exactly the same way as any user.
4. It is trivial to replace a facility or to provide a new one. The Kernel operates on data stored in tables. New facilities can be called by presenting the correct data entries. The decisions of the Kernel are not internal to the coding but are taken on the table entries.

The J level Supervisor is essentially multiprogramming. It not only multiprograms user programs but every one of its own facilities. Up to fourteen levels of user multiprogramming are permitted. It uses a straight priority system for determining which program to enter. The Supervisor facilities are given higher priority than user programs.

So far the internal structure has been discussed and this is of interest as it differs fundamentally from many Supervisors (or Executives, Directors, Master Routines etc) of other operating systems. Turning to the external view we now look at the facilities which it provides.

10.3.1 Operator Communications

The operator control station on System 4 consists normally of a console typewriter and certain other controls. If the machine is streamed, as will be described under Job Control, several control stations can be used. From type-ins from the console the operator controls the jobs that are running and is informed by the operating system of their status. Actions which the system requires from the operator are typed out, such as the loading of discs or magnetic tapes. The routine which controls the activities of the console acts asynchronously with the rest of the processing as it is essential that the relatively slow typewriter should not hold up the system. The messages are placed in a queue and this is continuously printed out at the typewriter speed. To reply to a query or to insert an option the typewriter interrupt is used and the reply can be inserted at any time.

A System Journal is kept on the disc of the log of the operation of the sysem. The Journal consists of one or more disc files which are available to an analysis program and are to be printed out.

10.3.2 Control of Input-Output

Control of input-output activities and file accessing comprises the largest part of the work of the Supervisor. All operations on a peripheral are considered as file activities, a deck of cards is a file, line printer output is a line printer file, and the data read or written to discs and magnetic tapes etc. is a file. Most files are labelled although this is not necessary. Before any peripheral is used the file must be opened. OPEN performs the functions of locating files, checking file

headers to verify that the file is the one requested by the user, positioning the file in the case of magnetic tape for example, setting up data blocks in the Supervisor showing the physical position of the file, marking files as open. The reverse operation CLOSE completes the accessing of a file and disengages the user from its use.
OPEN and CLOSE have a dual role. They grant permission for a user to utilise a peripheral device in some defined way. Only when the Supervisor has checked that the usage is permitted will the user have access to the file. Secondly they provide a user facility in that the user needs only to write in his program

OPEN FRED

for the file to be prepared for accessing and properly positioned. The name that appears in the program, FRED, is not the actual name of the file, that is, the name that appears on the magnetic tape or disc. It is termed the Symbolic Filename and is the name that is used internally to the program. Only at job run time is the internal name linked to the name of an actual file.

After a file is opened the Supervisor has many problems to solve.

(a) Is the input-output transfer request valid? Is it to a device that the user has permission to use?
(b) Transfers must be queued if they relate to a device which is sharing a channel.
(c) Transfers to random access files must be checked to ensure that they are directed to an area which is within the file extent.
(d) A successfully terminated transfer must be reported back to the user and if a further transfer is queuing for the use of the input-output channel it must be fired off.
(e) A transfer terminated by a fault, for example a data parity, requires recovery action. Magnetic tape and disc transfers are repeated a number of times. Disc failures require particularly careful handling to prevent errors due to dust causing permanent damage to the surfaces. A certain number of tracks of a disc can be declared faulty and alternative tracks can be allocated to take their place. The Supervisor has the task of switching the transfer from the faulty to the good track.

The J level system allows magnetic tape and disc volumes to be mounted on any free unit and the operating system automatically recognises the volume from the volume label and not from the unit number.

So far only the devices local to the processor have been mentioned. The remote communication devices, such as teletypes, video displays, terminals, etc., are handled through a routine known as the Communication Control Package which is an optional part of the Supervisor. The Supervisor creates an interface to the user program which hides the individual characteristics of the device. Many of these devices are attached by shared lines, such as polled or multidrop connections. The user, through this package, is presented with a simple data transfer to and from any device.

10.3.3 Program Actions

When a programming error forces Supervisor to be entered, such as when an illegal operation code is obeyed or an addressing error is met, the Supervisor dumps the user's registers and enters what is known as a STXIT routine. This is a routine which is provided by the user in his program and which will analyse the error and in some cases allow the job to continue. The user can present three addresses:

1. A recoverable error routine. The user is allowed to reenter his program.
2. An unrecoverable error routine in which the user is expected to close his job in an orderly fashion.
3. An operator communication routine. If this is supplied the machine operator can converse at any time with the running program by interrupting the machine from the console and by typing in a message addressed to the job.

The operating system allows for a program to consist of many overlays, each known by a segment number. The Supervisor contains a Loader which brings these into store. The segments have a minor amount of relocation to be performed on them.

Checkpoint facilities are built into the Supervisor so that any program may request a checkpoint record to be taken. A record is then taken of the current state of the job and the core image is saved on backing storage. Subsequently the job can be started from this record by requesting a RESTART through job control.

All jobs finish by calling the End of Job routine or by being forced into it by the system following a program failure. Any files left open are closed, any devices and the core store used by the job are released for rescheduling and messages and statistics are output to the operator's console and to the System Journal. The release of facilities is performed by a routine known as Deallocator which calls the routines for attempting to load another job from the queue which is set up by the job control routines.

10.3.4 Generation of the Supervisor

The process of producing a Supervisor modelled for an installation is known as System Generation. The complete system is issued by the manufacturer on a magnetic tape (or if the site is without a magnetic tape it will be issued on a disc). From this complete issue the System Generation process produces the version of the Supervisor on the discs which are nominated by the site to be the new System Discs. The following are the main adaptations which can be made in this process. These are made by reading a set of data cards which describe the required system.

1. The Supervisor tables are set up to reflect the machine configuration, that is, the number and position of the peripheral devices, the size of the main store, the description of the use of these and in particular the stream definitions which are required for job control. (The concept of streaming will be expanded under 10.5 Job Control.)
2. Optional facilities can be inserted, from minor facilities to the use of more than one control station or the inclusion of the Communications Control Package.
3. The number of levels of multiprogramming to be permitted are set, also the relative priorities of the facilities of the Supervisor. These priorities define the multiprogramming of the Supervisor routines.
4. Supervisor routines optionally can be permanently resident or read in as overlays (some for logical reasons have to be resident). The resident routines are selected and the number of overlay areas is set.

10.4 The Data Management System

It has already been stated that each complete set of data which can be read from or written to a peripheral device is regarded as a file. The control of file processing can be divided as follows.

1. The declaration within the program of the type of file and of the mode of access required for it. This declaration is known as the File Definition Table and is declared by a mnemonic such as DTFSR (Define The File for Serial Records). The Symbolic Filename is the left hand label to the File Definition Table.
2. The coding which translates logical requests for data management to physical commands to the Supervisor.
3. The Job Control cards which link the Symbolic Filename to the name of an actual file.
4. The Supervisor control which ensures that each transfer is legal and that the channel capacity is correctly allocated to each user.

The Data Management system is included in a program in the following way. The user declares in his program various File Definition Tables, in general one for each file which he wishes to access. After all the DTF tables have been declared the user inserts the macro call DTFEN. When the Usercode Assembler meets this macro it expands it to include all the coding that is necessary to satisfy the options declared by the previously defined File Definition Tables. In the case of high level languages a method is used which is more transparent to the user but it incorporates much the same type of system internally.

The complexity of the operations which are possible using these File Control Packages is largely a function of the type of device which is addressed. The operations on the random access devices are most complex of all and the four methods of access are described as an example.

1. *Physical Handling* (*DTFPH*)
   In this mode the user does all the work of creating the Command Chains and despatching them to the Supervisor using the EXDP (Execute Disc Program) macro call.
2. *Serial Records* (*DTFSR*)
   The file can consist of fixed or variable length blocks of data and each block can contain fixed or variable length records. The user, having declared the format of the file in the File Definition Table, accesses the records in a serial order by the use of such macros as GET and PUT.
3. *Direct Access* (*DTFDT*)
   This is the mode of access where the user can access the physical blocks of data in either a random or a sequential manner. The Command Chains necessary for disc transfers can be highly complex but in this mode they are constructed for the user who need only be aware of the logical location of data within the file.
4. *Indexed Random and Sequential Processing* (*DTFIS*)
   Logical records can be accessed either randomly, or sequentially from an initial record, not by means of their physical position but by means of key values held in the record itself. This handling method allows records not only to be read, but also to be updated, new records to be inserted in their key value position, and records to be deleted.

The Data Management System is such that users have the option to physically handle their data, or to handle it purely on a record by record basis and let the operating system take care of its physical location.

Using the more sophisticated handling, where it is logically possible to do this, a program becomes independent of the physical identity of the data and can be used on more than one type of device.

In describing the filing system, only conventional files have been treated up to now. These are known as Dedicated files as in general the area occupied by them is dedicated to their use and they occupy contiguous space or at least blocks of contiguous space. Internally to the system a further disc filing system is used, known as DTFPA (Define The File for Partitioned Access), which dynamically, track by track, acquires and releases space. System files whose content is required for a very short time tend to be of this nature, continually expanding or contracting in space. These files are termed Non-Dedicated, and while they are exclusive to the system in J-level, they are made available to the user under the Multijob and R level operating systems. A Non-Dedicated file consists of a chained set of tracks, linked together by information on the tracks themselves.

Under J level the free tracks are recorded in a 'bit list'. All Trials System files are of this type and for this reason the continual updating of versions of programs under test does not cause fragmentation problems on the discs.

10.5 Job Control

The control of users' jobs is broken down into several distinct routines:

1. *Job Input*
   This routine accepts the job descriptions read from the card reader, or paper tape reader, and stores the data on the system discs.
2. *Scheduler*
   This routine is called as soon as any complete job description is read or when any spare machine capacity becomes available, such as store or peripherals. It scans the list of jobs held on the system discs in a priority order which will be described to see whether another job is available to load in the machine.
3. *Allocator*
   When Scheduler has found a job to load, the actions of assigning the main storage and the peripherals to it are performed by Allocator. Allocator calls upon the Supervisor for the job to be loaded and then leaves it to the run time control of Supervisor. Scheduler is recalled to see whether any other jobs can be entered in the machine.
4. *Deallocator*
   This is entered when machine capacity is released, such as at the end of a job or when no further operations are required on a device. Scheduler is called following its action.

The J-level Job Control will supervise the automatic loading of over 100 jobs. The order of loading and the priority system which is used is controlled by the concepts of *Streams*, *Rank*, and *Priority*. A *stream* is a division of the machine in terms of main store, peripherals, and optionally of an operator control station. The machine may be divided into from one to six streams. No job may exceed the size of the stream for which it is declared, that is, jobs may not straddle streams. However any number of jobs may be run within each stream. In practice some users have only one stream in which case any one job may use all the facilities of the machine, while other users rigorously stream all jobs and the machine is used as several almost distinct systems.

Each job is designated a *Stream* (A–F), a *Rank* (0–9), and a *Priority* (1–14). The *rank* controls the order in which jobs are selected for running from within a stream. It may happen when several jobs are waiting to be run from a stream that a lower rank job will fit the available allocation of store and peripherals before a higher rank job. In general when this occurs the rank of a job which is passed over is upgraded by one until the maximum rank of nine is reached. A rank 9 job is forced into a stream. As soon as any store or any peripheral which it requires is released by deallocation it is donated to the rank 9 job. In this way a rank 9 job is run as soon as possible and as most other jobs rise in time to rank 9 no job can be permanently passed over or lost in the system. Ranks 0 and 1 have special meanings. Rank 0 is used for dormant jobs as it is a rank that is never updated and also no job in it is ever selected for running. It is used for running a sequence of jobs as the rank of a job can be altered by the operator or from a Supervisor call from a program under execution. A sequence of jobs can be inserted into Job Input the first of which has a 'proper' rank and the others have rank 0. The later members of the sequence are brought into action by changing the ranks according to the execution of the running jobs. Rank 1 is special in that it is never updated, and the Scheduler does not try to accommodate the second rank 1 job until the first is allocated. Rank 1 jobs are entered in the machine in their strict arrival order.

The streaming and ranking concepts are complex but sufficiently flexible to satisfy most requirements. Only a very few users would be expected to utilise six streams and all ten ranks. Many users would be satisfied with one single stream and all jobs submitted at rank 1, in which case the jobs would be allocated to store in the order of presentation of Job Input.

The *priority* rating (1–14) is a measure of the priority the job requires when running under multiprogramming. Priority 14 is the highest priority of the user programs.

10.6 The Trials System

The Trials System is the single system under which all the packages which assist the construction of programs are run. The system is a normal user job and is called to be run through Job Input with the directive JOB TRIALS. The main elements of the system are the *Amender*, the *Assembler* and *Compilers*, and the *Composer*. All trials data is held on the discs including the source text. A program is built in four stages.

1. Source Text or *Source Module*
2 .Compiled form or *Object Module*
3. Composed form or *Loadable Program Segment*
4. Loaded form as placed in core by the Loader

Source Modules are retained on disc in card format (multiple spaces are compressed) and the *Amender* program services these files to replace, insert, add, and delete cards. A source module when serviced by a Compiler (Fortran, Algol, Cobol, Cleo are available) or by the Usercode Assembler produces an *Object Module* which is not a core image form but a form which is suitable for composing together with other object modules to form a program. An object module is capable of relocation and also has external references unsatisfied. Theoretically any two modules written in any language can be composed together. However this can only be done between modules written in different high level languages by obeying strict conventions.

The *Composer* has as its data a list of object modules to join together and also a map of the structure that is required for the complete program. Overlaying free structures may be declared. Each unit of loading that is constructed is termed a *Loadable Program Segment*. These segments have all external references resolved and only address constants are not in their final form. Before the program can be run these relative addresses have to be updated to absolute store location values. This is done in the segment loading process which is performed by the Loader routine of Supervisor.

System 4 programs are written as a set of source modules. When a program is under test it is not necessary to compile the complete program every time. Only one module is amended and compiled and the loadable program is created by composing the amended module with the previously compiled modules. With high level language programs the input-output packages and the standard routines are included in the program as precompiled object modules and are brought in by the composition process. There are also several options for including standard test packages such as Snapshot, Trace, and Trial Data Fanout at Compose time. Trial Data Fanout sets up temporary files on magnetic tape or disc for program testing purposes.

10.7 Conclusion

From the description of J level it should be clear to the reader that it differs very much in its philosophy from the systems of the 1900 series. If another system had been chosen exactly the same thing would be true. The reader is left to draw his own comparisons. The present state of the art of designing them is such that all the virtues and some of the vices of all previous systems are brought together to form the next one, and in consequence general purpose operating systems are growing larger and larger, and taking more and more execution time and storage. The original design documents for OS360 included almost every known operating system concept of that time. At the same time general purpose systems have become harder and more complicated to use, in some cases with a job control card deck an inch or an inch and a half thick. A return to simplicity is required. The facilities must be there, but they must not make the system hard to use, they must be transparent, and their complications must only be known to those who wish to use advanced facilities.

THE CONTRIBUTORS

Angus Beatty was educated at Millfield, Stowe, and St. John's College, Cambridge. He first came across computers at English Electric in Stafford. He joined International Computers and Tabulators (later International Computers Ltd.) in 1963, and since then has planned and implemented the compile-time environmental aspects of the 1900 COBOL compiler, and headed the 1900 PL/1 Study Group.

Peter Burkinshaw was born in Wakefield in 1935. He was educated at Queen Elizabeth Grammar School, Wakefield, and Manchester University, where he graduated in mathematics. He was employed by Rolls-Royce at Derby on a wide variety of software projects from 1956 to 1964. After working briefly for IBM U.K. Laboratories on PL/1 he joined ICT in 1965 as Section Leader responsible for the design and implementation of the GEORGE 1 and 2 Operating Systems for the 1900 series computers. He is currently manager of Assembly Languages at ICL's Bracknell establishments.

Geoffrey Cuttle was educated at Malvern College, and Downing College, Cambridge. He joined the British Tabulating Machine Co. (now ICL) in 1956, and after three years as an instructor at their Bradenham Manor training school transferred to software development. He held various management positions on 1300, 1500 and 1900 series work and in 1967 became assistant to the then software organization manager, Mr P. M. Hunt. Subsequent to the formation of ICL he transferred to Corporate Planning Organization and is now Manager of the Software Specification Division.

David Foster is Manager of the ALGOL branch in Systems Programming Southern Division, ICL. He graduated in 1957 from Wadham College, Oxford, with an honours degree in mathematics. After a short spell with the de Havilland Aircraft Company he joined Ferranti Ltd, in 1959 as a programmer. He worked on the EMA compiler for Orion and later led the team which designed and implemented the EMA compilers for the ICL 1900 series. His present responsibilities include ALGOL compilers and conversational compilers for the 1900 series.

Timothy Goldingham, a former Classical Scholar of Christ Church, Oxford, began his data processing career with the British Tabulating Machine Co. in 1953. After working on electronic calculators in their Bristol office he moved in 1958 to Birmingham where he was trained as a programmer on the Hollerith 1202 computer.

After BTM became ICT he worked in a regional computer team installing 1300, 1500 and 1900 computers. He became manager of a software support group in 1964 and in 1967 moved to the Head Office in Putney where he now manages ICL's 1900 Software Support Department.

Stuart Miller worked for several years on program loaders and executive systems for various ICL computers. He joined the Real-Time Computer Branch of BEA, which implemented an executive for the UNIVAC 490 Real-Time Reservation System. His responsibilities included maintenance of the integrity of the on-line system, cutover to remote site reservations operations, and investigations into the conversion to 494 Central Processors. He then joined ICL as Manager of a branch conducting reserach into the requirements of a real-time executive for 1900 and System 4 machines. A complete software system was designed.

He is currently with UNIVAC leading the research and development function of a real-time software project.

Brian Millis graduated in mathematics from King's College, Cambridge in 1955, and studied computing using EDSAC 1, obtaining a diploma. From 1956 to 1961 he worked on general purpose software with the N.R.D.C., and after two years with EMI was transferred to International Computers' Stevenage Laboratory to develop the first 1902 Executive. Since then he has been in charge of development programming, including Executives, small and medium operating systems, satellite control and engineering test programs. He is currently Manager of a Programming Branch in the Data Processing Equipment Organization of ICL.

Philip Robinson was educated at Portsmouth Grammar School and Corpus Christi College, Cambridge, where he was a Classical Scholar. He spent nine years in India as a produce exporter and joined ICT in 1962. He worked on COBOL compilers for the 1301, 1500 and 1900 series computers, leading teams responsible for the Analysis Phase, Copy Phase and User Liaison. He is at present a Technical Officer with ICL at Reading.

Martin Warwick graduated in mathematics in 1955 and then spent a year in research in modern algebra. He entered the computer industry by joining English Electric Computers after a period of teaching. He was one of the chief designers of the System 4 Operating Systems, in particular the J Level Supervisor. His later work has been in the design of multi-access and other advanced systems, and he is at present manager of Advanced Systems Department, Sales Development Organisation of International Computers Ltd.

SELECTED BIBLIOGRAPHY

Operating Systems George 1 and 2, Mark 6 (*International Computers Ltd.* First edition 1968).

Operating Systems George 3 and 4, (*International Computers Ltd.* Second Edition, 1968).

Disc Operating System J Level, Vols 1 and 2 (*International Computers Ltd.*).

OS/360 Concepts and Facilities (*International Business Machines Ltd.*).

UNIVAC 494 Real-Time System Central Processor General Reference Manual (*UNIVAC Division of Sperry-Rand Corporation*).

UNIVAC 494 STARS Functional Description Manual (*UNIVAC Division of Sperry-Rand Corporation*).

ICL 1900 Series: Jean Manual (*International Computers Ltd.*).

RUSH Terminal User's Manual, 1966 (*Allen-Babcock Computing Inc.*).

JOSS: Introduction to the System Implementation *by* G. E. Bryan (p–3486, *The Rand Corporation*, 1966).

JOSS Language: Memorandum RM–5377–PR *by* G. E. Bryan *and* J. W. Smith (*The Rand Corporation* 1967).

On-Line Debugging Techniques: a survey *by* Thomas G. Evans *and* D. Lucille Darley (*Proceedings—Fall Joint Computer Conference*, 1966).

The Impact of Multiaccess *by* H. D. Baecker (*Computer Bulletin*, March 1968).

JOSS, a designer's view of an experimental on-line computing system, *by* J. C. Shaw (*Proceedings—Fall Joint Computer Conference*, 1964).

GEORGE 3—A General Purpose Time-Sharing and Operating System *by* M. D. Oestreicher, M. J. Bailey *and* J. L. Strauss (*Comm. A.C.M.*, Nov. 1967).

Proceedings of the A.C.M. Symposium on Operating System Principles, Gatlinburg, Tennessee, Oct. 1967, published in *Comm. A.C.M.* vol. 11, No. 5, May 1968, and including:

Resource Management for a Medium Scale Time-Sharing Operating System *by* G. Oppenheimer *and* N. Weizer.

The Working Set Model for Program Behaviour *by* Peter J. Denning.

The Structure of the 'THE' Multiprogramming System *by* Edsger W. Dikstra.

A Scheduling Philosophy for Multiprocessing Systems *by* Butler W. Lampson (resumé).

Dynamic Supervisors—their design and construction *by* D. H. R. Huxtable *and* M. T. Warwick (resumé).

An implementation of a multiprocessing computer system *by* William B. Ackermann *and* William W. Plummer (resumé).

The Compatible Time-Sharing System: a Programmer's Guide *by* F. J. Corbato *et al.* (M.I.T. Press, 2nd edition 1965).

Programming Real-Time Systems *by* James Martin, (Prentice Hall 1965).

A General-Purpose File System for secondary storage *by* R. C. Daley *and* P. G. Neumann (*Proceedings AFIPS* 1965; *Fall Joint Computer Conference* vol. 27 Pt 1, pp 213–29).

The design of multiple-access computer systems: Part 1 *by* M. V. Wilkes (*Computer Journal*, May 1967).

The design of multiple-access computer systems: Part 2 *by* M. V. Wilkes *and* R. M. Needham (*Computer Journal*, Feb. 1968).

Datafair 1966 Report. Articles on real-time operation, esp. Why Real-Time? by S. Gill. (*Computer Bulletin*, Ju ne 1966).

Design of Real-time Computer Systems *by* J. Martin (Prentice Hall, 1967).

Programming Systems and Languages *ed.* S. Rosen (McGraw-Hill, 1967).

Introduction to System Programming *ed.* P. Wegner (Academic Press, 1965).

Time-sharing Computer Systems, *by* M. V. Wilkes (Macdonald, 1968).

INDEX